"Shannon Evans' tender and honest book reminds us all to put first things recognizably first. Find in this book a way to return to a loving way of life, exquisite mutuality, and a renewed sense of service that allows us to be reached by the poor. This book helps you … to be in the world who God is."

— **Father Greg Boyle, SJ**, founder and director of Homeboy Industries, the largest gang intervention program in the world, and author of *Tattoos on the Heart* and *Barking to the Choir*

"I believe that the Body of Christ in the twenty-first century is very unhealthy. We are limping in our walk toward eternity. In order for us to be healed, we need to draw close to Jesus in the sacraments and the Body of Christ in the poor, marginalized, and oppressed people of our world. *Embracing Weakness* provides a model through Shannon Evans's testimony on how we can continually receive and share the healing power of Jesus Christ in our walk toward eternity."

— **Father Joshua Johnson**, author of *Broken and Blessed*, podcast host of *Ask Fr. Josh*, and pastor of Our Lady of the Holy Rosary Catholic Church

"*Embracing Weakness* is truly transformative. For anyone who has ever hesitated to show weakness — and isn't that all of us, really? — Shannon Evans demonstrates the spiritual freedom that comes from being vulnerable. Even better, she shows how this vulnerability will transform not just ourselves, but our families, our communities, our Church, and the world. Evans is the real deal, a seeker who doesn't hesitate to share her own mistakes as well as the graces she's encountered along the way. This book pulses with wisdom, authenticity, and heart."

— **Ginny Kubitz Moyer**, author of *Taste & See: Experiencing the Goodness of God with Our Five Senses*

"'We have spent decades crafting our very existence around strength and success, yet the upside down kingdom blatantly refuses to play by the game we know best.' Shannon has packed beautiful and hard truths in these pages that have ripped me open, encouraged, and challenged me all at once. She has exquisitely woven story with teaching all wrapped in the humility of a seeker of justice and love. I will be returning to this text often in my own walk toward solidarity and incarnation."

— **Ike Ndolo**, songwriter and recording artist

"At a time when faith and power strain to weave themselves into one smooth garment, *Embracing Weakness* offers a humble, terrifying alternative: It is in the decay of self-pride that true abundance takes root. Melding vulnerable storytelling and a persistent return to Scripture, Evans' deft prose is a reminder that authentic ministry begins at our frayed ends. I wish I could put this book in the hands of every church leader, every wide-eyed revolutionary, and every ordinary neighbor."

— **Shannan Martin**, author of
The Ministry of Ordinary Places and *Falling Free*

"Through powerful words, prophetic witness, and the paradox of vulnerability, *Embracing Weakness* invites us to examine our own lives as we wrestle with life's biggest questions and faith's deepest mysteries. Weaving together stories from her marriage, parenting, and ministry, Shannon Evans celebrates the beauty born from brokenness and the hope found in humility, beckoning us gently into conversion as she shares her own. Encountering God in the least likely places and faces, Shannon shows us how to embrace an incarnational faith in the mess and muck of everyday life. For anyone who's secretly wondered, 'Am I the only one?' or struggled to find God when everything falls apart, Shannon assures us we aren't alone. *Embracing Weakness* is a story of faith transformed and questions lived — a story for all of us."

— **Laura Kelly Fanucci**, author of *Living Your Discipleship:
7 Ways to Express Your Deepest Calling* and
Grieving Together: A Couple's Journey through Miscarriage

"Provocative and challenging. *Embracing Weakness* is a strikingly honest story about the struggle to live a more real and incarnational following of Jesus — being poor with the poor One. This book is a timely invitation to shed the masks of a 'clean-cut' Christian life. In allowing Jesus to enter into the mess of our own lives, we receive grace and courage to enter the mess of the world with Him. A beautiful and radical journey of ongoing conversion."

— **Father Emmanuel Mansford,**
Franciscan Friar of the Renewal, New York City

"Reader, be prepared to journey with Shannon Evans into 'the best of times and the worst of times.' Originally, she had a fixed image of herself, a fixed universe she would help save, a fixed faith that she would practice, and a fixed God who would save her. As life unfolds and she unravels, she matures in faith and her expectations of life. She grows in ways she did not expect; chief of these is growing to understand how her weaknesses can be secret sources of newfound strength. Jesus and his life are the examples she falls back on to solidify this new perspective on life. All the 'opposites' she had imagined before, now complement her life and ministry. She realizes that our weaknesses link us together. They are a natural bonding agent that builds intimacy between peoples. Her original desire was an illusion and when the veil was removed, she had to learn to live with the reality of the rubble that looked her straight in the eye. Moreover, to her credit, and to the gift of faith, from all this, she rises to new life. She even finds redemption in the rubble!"

— **Sister Jo-Ann Iannotti, OP,**
poet, photographer, author of *Remember, Return, Rejoice: Journeying from Ash Wednesday to Easter Sunday*

"With humility and authenticity, Shannon gently galvanizes us to embrace our weaknesses as well as our neighbors, revealing how doing one is really the work of the other. This book is a merciful and powerful invitation to become fully human, giving us all permission to embrace our tender spots so we may get on with the mission of changing the world."

— **Kayla Craig and Lindsy Wallac**e,
founders and co-hosts, *Upside Down* Podcast

Embracing
Weakness

The Unlikely Secret to Changing the World

Shannon K. Evans

**Our
Sunday
Visitor**

www.osv.com
Our Sunday Visitor Publishing Division
Our Sunday Visitor, Inc.
Huntington, Indiana 46750

Our Sunday Visitor Publishing Division
Our Sunday Visitor, Inc.
200 Noll Plaza
Huntington, IN 46750
1-800-348-2440

ISBN: 978-1-68192-266-9 (Inventory No. T1957)
eISBN: 978-1-68192-267-6
LCCN: 2019935180
Cover design: Chelsea Alt
Cover art: Shutterstock
Interior design: Amanda Falk
Interior art: Shutterstock

PRINTED IN THE UNITED STATES OF AMERICA

For Eric,
there but for the grace of you go I

Contents

INTRODUCTION

Once upon a time I was a missionary in Southeast Asia.

When my new husband and I joined the team, I magnanimously thought of what great good I would bring to the world (through the power of Christ, of course, *ahem*). I would work to stop human trafficking, I decided, though I had no connections in the field. I would pour myself into the lives of orphans, I predicted, though I had no idea where to start. I didn't worry about the details; after all, I served a God who would supply me everything I needed. I signed up for thrills, but got the monotony of regular old life instead.

After months turned into a year and the pages of the second year began flying off the calendar, I reviewed my life in despair. Nothing was going the way I had planned. Two years before, ripe and eager in the missions training school, I could never have expected to be so disappointed in myself. I could never have anticipated how small and ineffectual I would feel. My dreams had been way, way over my head — and now disillusionment was eating me alive. I knew I had to do something, anything, or my despair would swallow me whole.

I didn't have a background in ballet, but I did have access to YouTube tutorials, and I decided that was enough to teach a dozen of my elementary school-aged neighbors once a week. The diminutive girls in our low-income *kampung* (village) beamed and buzzed at the prospect of doing something so decidedly upper class. When a donor in the States sent money for ballet shoes, the buzz turned to a roar as little hands clamored to find their size. Two of the girls, sisters, were missing several toes — a genetic abnormality, I supposed. I wondered if they, more than others, were hungry to slide into soft pink leather. Maybe not. Perhaps I was the only one uncomfortable with my own deficiencies. Maybe these girls were content with themselves in a way I would work years to become.

The class was humble to say the least. We never even had a recital. But every Friday afternoon they would come, a tiny conglomerate of skinny brown limbs. Before mirrors and before the witness of one another, we would together admire the grace we didn't know we had. They, the grace to *plié* and *jeté* and see their own beauty while doing it; I, the grace of having less to offer than I thought, yet enjoying other people more than I ever had.

You see, I had never wanted to be weak: to be disappointed by my own lack of abilities or wounded by the suffering I would experience in life. In fact, for the first quarter of my life, I had successfully managed to fool myself into thinking I wasn't weak. Holding fast to religious absolutes, leadership positions, service projects, and a life of comfort, I went about my days quite satisfied in the knowledge that I was one of the good guys. I pseudo-benevolently offered to embrace the weakness of others all day long, but I refused to reconcile with my own — that is, until the truth of my inner brokenness smacked me in the face, first through missions and immediately afterward, through motherhood.

I suspect I'm not alone in this. I think, deep down, each of us knows we aren't as strong as we appear to be. The ever-growing list of our failures, disappointments, and sufferings is never far from our minds. And rather than deal with the harsh realities life has served up, we find more pleasant ways of coping: food and drink, incessant exercise, romantic relationships, volunteer hours, or the consumption of media and material goods, just to name a few. We can numb our pain with the elements sold to us as "the good life" and temporarily forget that we are not who we'd like to imagine ourselves to be. This feels harmless, until the day we wake up to the reality of the damage caused by our unwillingness to do the hard work of inner change: dealing with emotional distance in our closest relationships, undignified treatment of those we claim to serve, and even a marred understanding of the nature of God.

Subtle messages of power and "rightness" have infiltrated our theology and churches so much that we don't even recognize how distorted is the view of God they propagate — an incarnation-less God who has no real compassion for or solidarity with the people of the world he claims to love. Humankind has a fatal tendency to make God into our own image, and if we can't authentically draw near to those who are not like us, we begin to subconsciously believe God cannot draw near to them either.

The further out of touch we become with our own weakness, the more we distance ourselves from anyone outside of our particular "correct" bubble of faith. We dutifully seek to meet the needs of the world while denying that those outside our bubble might actually be able to meet ours. In neglecting to first embrace our own weakness before addressing the weakness of others, we lose the value of reciprocity that Jesus modeled so profoundly. We miss the gift of receiving a sacred God through vessels we have deemed unworthy.

Jesus, on the other hand, didn't sort people into boxes labeled "acceptable" or "in need of ministry." When the God of heaven came to earth in human likeness, he chose unethical tax collectors, prostitutes, and low-income fisherman to be his closest friends. He told parables that cast an immigrant as the hero (the good Samaritan), a pious religious leader as the villain (the Pharisee and the tax collector), and a rich man as the fool (the rich fool). He offended social mores, breaking class and gender lines, and challenged the status quo. People called him "a friend of ... sinners" (Lk 7:34) and he wasn't embarrassed, nor did he correct them.

If we're honest, we can't deny that modern Christianity looks much different. Today Christians of all stripes are largely concerned with living clean lives of personal morality and feeling affronted by the secular culture around us. When we do attempt to follow Jesus' model of the works of mercy, there is a tangible sense of relief when the service is over and we can go back to online shopping and dinner at our favorite restaurant.

Yet we profess this faith because we believe in the way of Christ. Somewhere within us, we long for more. Despite the attraction of comfort and ease, we know we were created for something deeper.

Through his Incarnation and Passion, Jesus gave us the secret of a more meaningful life; and that secret, shockingly, is embracing our weakness. Rather than reigning from a palace and ruling with an iron fist as he could have done, Jesus came quietly, humbly — willingly accepting the disappointments, limitations, and sufferings of the human experience. The Eternal Word took on flesh so that we could be in full communion with God, without walls dividing the Divine experience from ours as humans. In the way of Jesus, we, too, are invited to make peace with the weakness of our humanity. We, too, are invited into a communion without walls.

For too long we have approached justice and evangelization through our interpretation of "rightness." Embracing our weakness frees us from this subtle reach for power to find our own reflection in the eyes of the marginalized or the face of the non-Christian. As we open ourselves to encounter God in our own places of pain, disappointment, and self-disillusionment, our judgments of others disintegrate. As we risk authentic encounter with the limitations and sorrow of our own humanity, we grow in empathy for those around us. This willingness to embrace our own weakness allows us to see fewer "projects" or "issues" and more individual human beings with stories of their own. It allows us to relate to those who are different with the reciprocity of Jesus, a posture of the heart that believes and expects all people — even and perhaps especially the least likely — to have something important to offer us, not merely vice versa.

When we are honest about our own pain and disappointments, we can experience the freedom that Jesus knew. This is a freedom that births solidarity and compassion with our fellow man, a freedom that allows the Spirit to inhabit our gaping holes and imbue our lives with meaning.

Our lives must be more examined and less self-medicated if we truly want to be communal, spiritually vibrant, and rich in mercy. Making the decision to stop numbing our pain and embrace transparency in our relationships does not mean our lives will be transformed overnight. But making this decision empowers us to commit to an ongoing conversion. Yes, this conversion will take all our lives, but there is no need to be daunted by the prospect — after all, this is what the Christian life is all about. The benefits are wholeness in our being, authentic relationships, and a world of more compassion and joy.

In the pages of this book, I share vulnerably about my own journey. Even while knowing that we each have been given our own stories, I confess that I hope you recognize a bit of your own in mine. We are traveling together, you and I, as are billions of other people on this planet, and we are none of us so very different after all. I offer you the greatest beauty and the most painful aching of my life thus far, and I ask that in exchange you might offer me an open heart. Embracing our weakness can be an uncomfortable endeavor, but Jesus beckons us beyond comfort, beyond control, beyond strength: to where only love remains. May we say yes and follow.

Chapter One

WHERE WE
GO WRONG

I sighed happily, closed the book in my lap, and gazed out the window. It was the perfect kind of day for a transcontinental flight. Cerulean sky and cirrus clouds affirmed my confidence that this was the path my life was always meant to take. I gave my husband a gentle elbow to the ribs and we exchanged grins. There had been a few tears at the airport between our families and us, but I was so excited I barely tasted the salt of them. *Missionaries*, I thought to myself. After two years of training, we finally got to wear the title. After a quarter-century search for meaningful adventure, my life was finally about to begin.

Sodas on airplanes always taste a little better than they do on the ground, and my small cup of Sprite was no exception. Sipping the bubbles, I picked up my book again and studied the cover. A middle-aged charismatic American missionary in Mozambique was pictured surrounded by African street kids. The fiery wife and mother of two was everything I dreamed of becoming. Her autobiography told of her work in the slums of Mozambique, where she had seen illnesses healed, the dead raised to life, and the traumatized hearts of orphans set free to love and worship God.

I couldn't envision a more desirable way to spend a life, and having traveled to Third World countries for short-term mission trips several times before, I wasn't intimidated by the sacrifices it would cost. We were being sent to Indonesia — not Mozambique — through the missions arm of our nondenominational church, but still I read my own hopes in black-and-white print somewhere over the Pacific Ocean.

My life was going to matter. I was going to be fearless, and I would see miracles. Yes, of course, if God willed it and all of that, but why wouldn't he? Looking around down here on earth, there didn't exactly seem to be a surplus of people willing to do the brave things that I was doing. I wouldn't say God needed me, but I wouldn't deny he was lucky to have me.

I reclined my seat back the eighth of an inch it was designed to go, happy determination in my heart. This was going to be a wild ride.

———————————

To be human is to carry around the companionship of an internal ache. Some of us have become so adept at ignoring this, that we deny it's present at all. But I would argue that most of us are willing to own up to the presence of a gnawing pain within. Dorothy Day famously dubbed it "the long loneliness," but it goes by other names, too: fear, shame, disappointment, disillusionment, weakness. Such deeply rooted motivators generally manifest in one of two ways: either they woo us into spells of depression, or they repel us so much that we spend our lives trying to run from them.

I, for one, am a runner. I seek to avoid my own weakness by trying to stay one step ahead of it, and at times it almost appears to be working, times that I can be steady as a rock. But inevitably a relationship will implode or a circumstance will break me, and then I have no choice but to confront my demons head-on. Or at least I imagine myself to be doing so, with a congratulatory pat on the back for my keen self-awareness and teachable spirit. Then, just as predictably, once the dust settles, I return to my numbed state of being. It's downright cyclical.

Differences in our personalities or temperaments aside, almost all human beings want to be seen as powerful and effective, not weak and needy.

But I know another manifestation — depression — too, and intimately. My husband, Eric, has been blessed with an artistic temperament, and I say that with utmost respect, because his high levels of consciousness and empathy have deeply shaped me. Yet such sensitivity comes with a price; he feels darkness and fragility often and acutely, and is more inclined than I to experience bouts of depression. He absorbs the ache; I run from it. But I've found one thing to be true to both experiences: no matter what your knee-jerk reaction is to your own poverty, none of us feels at ease welcoming it. Differences in our personalities or temperaments aside, almost all human beings want to be seen as powerful and effective, not weak and needy.

Admitting our lack to one another does not come naturally. Indeed, it's quite contrary to the self-preservation instinct that kicks in to keep us out of harm's way. Don't be vulnerable, our brains warn us. Don't let anyone in. You'll get hurt. It feels far safer to be seen as competent and esteemed. After all, if everyone really knew how small and disappointing you felt, how could they still respect you? How could you achieve your goals? How could you ever hope to matter in the world if your weaknesses were made known?

But it's not just our minds that send out flashing danger signals when it comes to getting honest about our own insides; it's our society, too: "Boys don't cry." "Never let them see you sweat." "Fake it 'til you make it."

Our fears are not exactly unsubstantiated. Looking at history, it was the powerful who "conquered" the land we now call the United States, and the powerful continue to be disproportionately rewarded here. The rich are exposed to boundless opportunity, while the poor are stuck in the riptides of poverty. Studies show that attractive people are paid as much as 13 percent more than their average-looking peers.[1] Respect is instinctively given to families whose marriages are intact and

---

1. Daniel Hamermesh, *Beauty Pays: Why Attractive People are More Successful* (Princeton, NJ: Princeton University Press, 2013).

whose children are the school "all-stars," even with no idea of what goes on behind their closed doors. They are the Joneses, and we are determined to keep up. Between our protective subconscious and our cultural messages, it's amazing that we ever open up to anyone at all, and confessing our own deepest ache to a confidant is certainly not something we do every day. Even meeting with a professional therapist, as beneficial as it may be, can potentially become a way to avoid vulnerable, organic relationships if we are not careful.

This lack of authentic connection creates a void inside the human person. Instinctively, we try to fill this space with other things. For most of us, it doesn't take much introspection to acknowledge our tendency to consume as compensation for weakness or loneliness. Whether food, drink, shopping, Netflix, recreational drugs, or something else entirely, we each have respective addictions that we are happy to let fill the role of honest relational intimacy in our lives. But the further we run down the rabbit hole, the harder it becomes to see clearly, until one day we are brutally woken up to all that we've lost in the spending.

The internal gnawing we feel of needing connection, so familiar to the human experience, has the potential to bring us together; vulnerability births intimacy, after all, if we're willing to go there. Such unity could be the very reason the Creator knit our bones and sinews into such an emotionally weighty reality. Unfortunately, statistics show that more of us feel greater isolation than ever before. In a 2016 interview with *Fortune Magazine*,[2] the director of the University of Chicago's Center for Cognitive and Social Neuroscience, John Cacioppo, said numerous studies confirm that Americans are only getting lonelier. This was corroborated by the 2018 findings of a nationwide survey administered by health insurer Cigna. Out of twenty thousand

---

2. Laura Entis, "Chronic Loneliness Is a Modern-Day Epidemic," *Fortune*, June 22, 2016, http://fortune.com/2016/06/22/loneliness-is-a-modern-day-epidemic/.

individuals surveyed, nearly half reported that they sometimes or always felt alone. What's more, 43 percent reported sometimes or always feeling that their relationships are not meaningful. These numbers are of epidemic proportions.

Statistics like these tell us the unity of connection isn't happening, but Scripture tells us that it could. The Book of Genesis describes man and woman as being made in God's own image, bearing the imprint of the Lord's likeness. If the most powerful encounter a human being can experience is with the Living God, would we not be fools to discount the potency of touching the *imago Dei* that stands right in front of us when we take off the masks and let one another in?

The weakness of the human condition is a gift given to us so that we may truly encounter God in what Jewish philosopher Emmanuel Levinas called "the other."[3] Despite how it sounds, the "other" is not a gruesome alien from outer space; it's simply a human being outside of oneself. But to take it one step further, let's say the other is specifically a human being who appears different from yourself in some way, for that distinction is often critical when it comes to our level of discomfort.

Young children need little prompting to handle this well; they are refreshingly inclined to make friends with those who are different. It's common for young parents to comment on the way their small child "doesn't see" skin color or other physical differences, often with the mystified pride of having created a rare inclusive individual. But far from being the exception, this is a universal quality of all children at a certain developmental stage.[4] Granted, perhaps your daughter is a particularly empathetic person, but the point here is that we have much to learn from all of our toddlers. Sadly, we seem to lose the ability to look past differ-

---

3. Emmanuel Levinas, *Humanism of the Other* (Champaign, IL: University of Illinois Press, reprint edition 2005, originally published 1972).

4. Marguerite A. Wright, "Appendix: Stages of Racial Awareness," in *I'm Chocolate, You're Vanilla: Raising Healthy Black and Bi-Racial Children in a Race-Conscious World* (San Francisco: Jossey-Bass, 1998).

ences as we age. We become wary of those who have not shared our particular life experiences — yet another reason Jesus urged us to change our hearts to become like a little child (cf. Mt 18:3). We must return to the humble, welcoming state of childhood to enter the kingdom of God.

Without a paradigm-altering confrontation with our own weakness, it is virtually impossible to feel true connection with the other on a significant level. If we are not in touch with our own smallness, our own sense of having fallen short of our hopes

> *We must return to the humble, welcoming state of childhood to enter the kingdom of God.*

and ideals, we will never be able to authentically touch someone else's vulnerability — the only place of true encounter. Instead, we will resort to power plays and intimidation games, and I'm not just talking about in the office or marketplace.

We put up walls around our hearts even against those we hold most dear. As we age, our relationships with our own parents can be the most difficult ones to maneuver. Often the same could be said of our adult siblings. Truly intimate friendships are rarer in adulthood than in childhood, as we become more comfortable operating out of self-sufficiency and grow less willing to express our emotional need for others. Marriage is, but for the grace of God, the most impossible relationship that we could ever have imagined. Parenthood is a breeding ground for control issues and fear. Estrangement of the heart is not relegated to disgruntled co-workers or the immigrant neighbor you feel too uncomfortable to really get to know. This instinct for self-preservation affects even the closest relationships in our lives.

We seek to operate from a place of power, because this makes us feel more protected from potential injury. We seek to control a relationship, whether through dominance or passive-aggression, because in this way we feel less likely to play the fool. But choosing these paths restrains us from the fullness of life that God desires for us. That fullness includes relationships that mine the depths of love, self-sacrifice that conforms us more to the image of our Savior, and inner change in all the ways we cannot see that we need.

For Christians who actively strive to live out their faith in the world, this human tendency to deny their own brokenness and grasp for power is subtler — and yet more dangerous — than they would like to believe. Instead of embodying a unitive humility, too many of us Christians instead spend a lot of time and volume on having all of the answers that others may or may not feel are important.

The painful truth is that our own weakness makes us uncomfortable, and the quickest way to ease that discomfort is to position ourselves in a place of power. If we're honest with ourselves, we may be forced to admit that our efforts to help are not really about authentic encounter with one another as much as they are about how good it feels to be the

It is all too easy to jump into ministries of evangelism or service with the unconscious motivation of feeling strong and useful.

one with the ability to offer solutions, whether material or theoretical. It is all too easy to jump into ministries of evangelism or service with the unconscious motivation of feeling strong and useful. Just as things like alcohol or shopping can be agents to numb the pain of our weakness, so too can ministry. In fact, it is perhaps the most perilous "fix" for a Christian, because it looks so good and altruistic that it's easy to fool ourselves into believing we are in it for the right reasons.

Perhaps this seems harmless enough, as far as vices go. But

when the curtain is pulled back, we see that ministry from a pedestal benefits no one: Not only does it diminish the dignity of those being served, but it chips away at our own humanity as well. When we are not in touch with the poverty of our own human condition, the work of ministry can fool us into thinking we have "arrived" and hence keep us from the wholeness that God desires for us. We continue to numb the places inside us where the Holy Spirit wants to come, and we deny ourselves the chance to see what riches the needy and marginalized have to offer.

This truth is not relegated to the works of mercy alone, but applies to our efforts of evangelism, too. Can we be honest about the pressure that comes with the word *evangelism* for a moment? Too many of us feel that, in order to be worthy of the title "evangelist," we must be on the victorious side of a struggle. The result is that we feel either smugly superior or categorically disqualified. The pressure is so intense that many well-meaning Christians refuse to evangelize at all, which is a shame.[5]

We need to seek a true understanding of what it means to evangelize, and that requires we come to a truer understanding of ourselves as evangelizers. Pope Francis has said, "Evangelization does not consist in proselytizing, but ... in humbly drawing near to those who feel distant from God and the Church, those who are fearful or indifferent, and saying to them: 'The Lord, with great respect and love, is also calling you to be a part of his people' (*Evangelii Gaudium*, 113)."[6] Evangelism is finding Christ already

> *The power of the Gospel is not that we no longer suffer or struggle, but that we no longer do so alone.*

5. Barna Group, "Sharing Faith Is Increasingly Optional to Christians," *Research Releases* in *Faith & Christianity*, May 15, 2018, https://www.barna.com/research/sharing-faith-increasingly-optional-christians/.

6. Homily at Mass in Quito's Bicentennial Park during visit to Ecuador, July 7, 2015.

present in the world, and inviting the other into the loving belonging of the inclusive family of God.

If my testimony of the gospel revolves around a plotline of, "I used to struggle with this, but God gave me the victory and now I'm free/healed/saved/fill in the blank," I have immediately distanced myself from the listener of my testimony by implying that I have arrived in a place where they are not. No doubt we do find freedom, healing, and salvation in Christ — and want that for others, too — but the reality continues to be that we ourselves are also in process. The power of the gospel is not that we no longer suffer or struggle, but that we no longer do so alone.

The Second Person of the Trinity stepped in to recorded history to relate intimately with humankind, so that in his willingness to share our lived experience he might gain our trust. This has to be the pattern of our efforts at evangelization and of any ministry we undertake. Can another person really trust us if we are not willing to bare our own weaknesses while prying into theirs? Are we, in our efforts of evangelization, asking something of the other that we ourselves are not ready to extend first?

Of course, many of us do not recognize that our hearts are in this place when we're trying to minister or evangelize. We certainly don't want them to be. But if we're willing to look closely, most of us have an "us and them" mentality, whether conscious or not.[7] This is marked by a discomfort with, avoidance of, or desire to change anyone who is not a part of the particular culture in which we are most comfortable. By "culture," I mean not only one's place of origin, but also things less often associated with the term, such as socioeconomic status, ethnicity, sexuality, and religious affiliation or lack thereof.

---

7. For an example, see Russell Heimlich, "Threat of Secularism to Evangelical Christians," Pew Research Center, *Fact Tank*, July 12, 2011, http://www.pewresearch.org/fact-tank/2011/07/12/threat-of-secularism-to-evangelical-christians/. While this research looks specifically at evangelical Christians, I think it is fair to say that many of the findings are broadly applicable to all of us.

As a nondenominational church-planting missionary in Indonesia, I had the best of intentions and a deep concern for the people around me, as did all the folks I knew who held similar roles. But in my nearly four years of training and serving, it was consistently communicated to me that my ultimate responsibility to every person I met was to try to lead them to a conversion experience with Christ. Such a worldview may seem harmless and even good, depending on your particular spirituality, but a closer look reveals the necessity of a line drawn in the sand. This mentality leads to the inadvertent creation of a "club," where one is either in or out.

In my experience, the approach seemed to be that cultivating deep friendships with non-Christians was valuable only if the individual seemed likely to convert. Sharing in their sufferings (and being vulnerable with them about my own) was lauded but, at the end of the day, not the ultimate goal, and thus not critically important.

In the stream of Christianity in which my husband and I belonged, the idea of relational evangelism was looked down upon. "You don't have to earn the right to share the gospel," a leader once told us. "Jesus already did that for you." Which — translated into its most honest but abrasive form — means you have the right to push your beliefs upon strangers without taking time to know them as human beings.

It could be argued that this is a tragic consequence of the "once saved, always saved" theology that undergirds many Protestant beliefs. Indeed, my world was turned upside down the day a gentle Anglican priest friend introduced the idea of salvation being a journey we are all walking on rather than a line in the sand that we have either crossed or not, and I came to find that my soul deeply resonated with the Catholic teaching of a continual salvation. But the truth is we Catholics have our own dragons to slay that don't look much different than those of our evangelical brothers and sisters.

Evangelicals focus on leading people to make a singular, eternal, life-altering decision. We Catholics don't have the same focus in our evangelizing efforts, but the same outcome-based mentality still plagues us, and we tend to operate within the same "us and them" paradigm. Aside from our efforts to spread the gospel, this also plays itself out in our ministry. We, along with many of our Protestant counterparts, undertake the works of mercy to meet people's physical needs, but the work is only temporary. We make no long-term emotional investment, which means there's very little at stake for us when we perform these works. We want our hearts to be conformed to Christ, but we also want the service project done on time so that we can keep our dinner date. It's important to ask ourselves honestly: How often do I perform acts of service to check them off a list, or because my faith says I have to, or because I like the pious feeling I get when I perform them?[8]

We know the Incarnation mysteriously unites all of humankind to God and one another, but so often the lines of Christianity feel like they do nothing but divide us.

Regardless of where we fall on the theological spectrum, in the depths of our spirits we know our faith is meant to be more than a one-time prayer that will save a sinner's soul, and more than meeting people's physical needs without fully engag-

8. For my Protestant friends who are reading, I feel the need to clarify a grave misconception. We Catholics do not believe we are saved by these works alone, but that true faith always goes hand in hand with action, as it says in James 2. A properly catechized Catholic understands this important distinction.

ing their hearts. This might be why so many Christians are frustrated and disillusioned with the Faith. We know the Incarnation mysteriously unites all of humankind to God and one another, but so often the lines of Christianity feel like they do nothing but divide us.

At the same time, we are each waging our own internal war against the weaknesses of our human condition, but we're too proud or too ashamed to admit them to anyone else — or, sometimes, even to ourselves. These two problems seem unrelated, but perhaps they couldn't be more intricately tied. Perhaps the very thing that is meant to unite us to the world around us has actually distanced us from it — and we don't know how to come back.

I walked the narrow alley back to our house, sandals shuffling dust underfoot, arms loaded with canvas bags filled with eggs and bread, oil and bananas. *"Mau pulang?"* The elderly woman a few doors down inquired with the polite warmth of a culture that prides itself on manners. "Are you going home now?"

I smiled, responded in the affirmative, and stopped to make small talk, reminding myself to be thankful for the spontaneous opportunity to practice my fledgling language skills. We had been in the *kampung* for eight months, and our Javanese neighbors were beginning to get used to the glowing white couple and our odd ways. Whether they were as happy to have us there as they seemed or the politeness of their culture had an iron will, we couldn't tell: The best we could do was hope for the former. This particular neighbor had struck me as the *kampung* gossip, and I always wondered what foreign words she used for me when her tongue ran away with her. Was there an Indonesian word for snob? Surely so, but I didn't yet know it. Perhaps if I did I would have kept an ear out.

When we moved into our little house in the *kampung*, we were thrilled to participate in the close-knit community life of a low-income Javanese neighborhood. At first, people came out of the woodwork to help move in the furniture we had bought in town or to bring us a hot meal. Eric and I had learned to adjust to life without hot water or a Western-style toilet or shower. Ignoring the *cicaks* (lizards) that constantly roamed our walls thanks to the permanently opened windows became second nature. I'm an animal lover, and geckos pose no threat. It was all going well, yet as the weeks ticked by, relationships had begun to lag. The language barrier was a problem, of course, but those things are overcome every day. This was something more.

The pressure to evangelize every person I met, the mission of converting hearts and minds, the lack of room for any true depth of mutuality in relationship, all felt like a suffocating weight I couldn't bear. Any effort to get to know someone was haunted by the underlying mandate that I fix what was broken in their lives. There was no room for brokenness of my own; I could quietly take that back to the people in my own corner.

I soon observed that my response was, little by little, to close myself off from everyone. My subconscious couldn't hold the tension between my failure to perform my job and the nagging feeling that the job itself was asking something of me that I didn't like. So, I withdrew. Day by day I pulled further inward, holing up in my tiny house to cook unnecessarily intricate recipes and watch movies rented almost daily from the local video store. Consumption was an opiate, an escape from the reality of my desert-dry heart, an escape from the disappointment within that felt too raw to touch. Where were those dreams of worship-

> *Consumption was an opiate, an escape from the reality of my desert-dry heart.*

ing street kids and redeemed orphans now? They felt like the hopeless naiveté of a girl from long ago. I willed my mind to return to the neighbor's chatter. Today was *Idul Adha*, she was informing me. I racked my brain and vaguely remembered: ah, yes, the feast of sacrifice. I had been taught about the Muslim holiday honoring Abraham's willingness to sacrifice his own son to the Lord, and the mercy of Allah to provide a ram in his stead. *A feast of mercy,* I thought to myself, *I could get on board with that.* I told her I would put away the groceries and return to walk to the mosque with her.

As we navigated our way through the alleys that made up our beloved neighborhood, a familiar heaviness weighed on my heart. This holy day was the perfect segue through which to present the gospel message: The parallels between the stories of Isaac and Jesus Christ are blatant and poignant, and anyone remotely interested in religion of any form would be keen to discuss it. It was an underhand soft pitch and all I had to do was swing.

But I kept silent.

We turned onto the only road in the *kampung* wide enough to fit a car, and I did a double take. There was a flash of red out of the corner of my eye, and was it what I thought? I squinted, then sucked in my breath as we stepped closer. Flowing, gushing, running through the open drains that lined the streets of our neighborhood was an unmistakable stream of siren-red blood. Blood mixed with water, in fact, as though it had come flowing straight from Christ's pierced side. I felt him there, suddenly, a heavy presence; I felt him nearer than he'd been in a long, long time.

We walked further and joined the mass of neighbors gathered for the annual animal sacrifice. Goats and cows dotted the landscape, some alive and some no longer. Men and women grinned proudly to show me what they had brought to offer. Boys and girls ran amok, happily weaving in and out of hanging carcasses. To me, it was a bloodbath. To them, it was a feast of mercy.

I could only bring myself to stay for a little while before walking the path home alone. A knot made its way up my throat as I closed my front door. Falling to my knees, I began to sob without even being sure why. The Lamb of God who takes away the sin of the world had already come, and they either didn't know or didn't believe: My years of missionary training told me that was why I wept. If they died today, they would be headed for the fires of hell: My ultraconservative faith formation told me that was why I wept. But neither felt true; neither felt sufficient to explain the aching in my heart, the grief that I knew was from Christ but for which I had no language. It wasn't until years later that I would put my finger on what I felt that day. I cried heaving tears on cool tile not because my neighbors didn't know Jesus the way I did. I cried because I didn't know them like he did.

Chapter Two

NUMBING
AGENTS

My feet were giddy as I stepped into the welcome air conditioning of the Western-style mall. We had driven an hour and a half from our much smaller town just south of Surabaya to this large Southeast Asian metropolis. We needed nothing here but familiarity, which was more than enough of a reason to make the road trip.

Without pausing to consult one another, my husband and I instinctively turned the corner to nab a place in line at Starbucks like a pair of caffeine-deprived synchronized swimmers. I didn't even drink coffee, but when you're in search of Americanized comfort in a shopping mall, your quest is not complete without a green mermaid on a cup. Minutes later, nursing our respective drinks, we commenced a luxurious day of window shopping. Maybe we would buy a pair of overpriced jeans. Maybe a tennis racket. Maybe we'd catch a movie in a theater that wasn't run-down. The world was our oyster for one glorious weekend, and everywhere we looked we found reminders of much longed-for home and comfort.

We loved our town in the mountains of the tropics, but there was very little that was comfortable or comforting about it: a Pizza Hut, a McDonald's, an Ace Hardware (yes, really). We did have a mall of decent proportion, but it was stocked wall-to-wall with distinctly Asian stores and sizes, which meant it couldn't be relied upon to bail us out of a case of the homesick blues. Day in and day out we were surrounded by reminders of our own foreignness, so when we needed reprieve, we frequently took weekend trips out to Surabaya to refresh ourselves. It didn't matter that 99 percent of the city was as traditionally Indonesian as the rest of the country; all that mattered was that it was home to that stalwart emblem of the American good life — a large mall.

As uncomfortable as we get when identifying our own weakness, that feeling is exponentially multiplied when we are asked to take stock of the coping mechanisms we use to deal with that internal poverty of our faults. No one wants their vices unearthed, even if it's only ourselves looking. Better to let those vices fly under the radar, we think. Better to wink them off as bad habits. *What can you do? We've all got 'em!*

But the numbing agents in our lives — the addictions or compulsions we use to keep negative feelings at bay and avoid having to confront our pained and vulnerable places — only send us deeper down the rabbit hole. They don't address the reasons for our aches in the first place, and certainly don't heal them. What's worse, when we choose not to feel our poverty, we miss out on seeing the full nature of Christ, not to mention experiencing true communion with our fellow man. A heart deadened to its own struggle can never be a refuge for the struggles of others.

> *When we choose not to feel our poverty, we miss out on seeing the full nature of Christ.*

A list of faithful numbing agents is a mile long, but we can start by identifying the obvious ones, those socially recognized addictions to things like alcohol, sex, pornography, and drugs. The thing about these looming categories is that most of us know they are harmful. If we're struggling in any of these areas, we are likely already seeking help or at least feeling guilty about it. As Christians, we know the effects of these addictions are serious, and so we take them seriously.

But what about the areas that are a bit more gray? What about things like food, shopping, exercise, social media, or the Internet in general? Many of us start to squirm when the word "addiction" is assigned to these very familiar, seemingly innocent, parts of our lives. Those topics as potential pitfalls are getting just a little too close to home. But like it or not, research studies are increasingly finding that these seemingly innocuous things are far more potentially addictive than we think. When we do something that feels good, whether posting a photo that gets hundreds of "likes" or buying a new shirt on a whim, we get a rush of the neurotransmitter dopamine. That in and of itself is not bad, but it does require us to wield the privileges of things like Facebook and credit cards responsibly, because with time and repetition we build up a chemical tolerance that keeps us wanting more — much like the experience of a drug addict needing a fix.

Of course, not all of us are bearing the weight of an actual addiction (although I would argue more of us are than we realize). But most of us are laboring against very real attachments that have a greater hold on us than we realize. We all use certain mediums to varying degrees as buffers from the disappointments, failures, sins, and shortcomings with which we would otherwise be confronted. Because the easiest way to stop feeling the effects of a gaping hole is not to seek to heal it — which requires a lot of hard work — but to fill it with something.

I'll offer myself as an example.

I am home with my children and have become absolutely itchy with restlessness. I'm making peanut butter sandwiches for the ninety-eighth time this week, and inside I am thinking of the extensive list of things I'd rather be doing. I love my children, but raising them is small, menial work; it very rarely feels significant (though I understand that it is), and even more rarely brings out flattering elements of my personhood. Today I am facing down my impatience, resentment, and sloth — and I am losing. This reality is not comfortable for me, so almost unconsciously I make the executive decision to move our entire operation to a location that *is*.

And so we enter Target for the second time this week. I get

a latte, the kids get apple juice and popcorn, and I roam around the red-and-white paradise knowing I have about forty-five glorious minutes until the magic begins to fade for my comrades. I am able to refrain from spontaneously buying anything this time, but just the knowledge that it's here for the taking if I want it is enough to get me through the afternoon. Under the preternatural lights of Target, even buying a box of diapers is satisfying, and so I am content putting those alone in my cart.

Walking through the aisles of fluffy towels that are not only softer than mine at home but also the exact shade of lavender I hadn't realized I'd wanted ten minutes prior, I am suddenly nicer to my kids. I'm suddenly a happier person — pleasant, even, with no sign of a hot temper or an inclination to yell on a dime. I don't feel quite so lonely now. No longer am I plagued with thoughts of whether I'm making a difference in the world or why no one appreciates me. Everything suddenly feels okay again. Target has done its job.

This scenario could have gone a hundred different ways: Sometimes in my personal narrative Target is replaced by Chick-fil-A, sometimes by online shopping, sometimes by scrolling through Instagram or digging into the ice cream at 11:00 a.m. The destination may change, but my commitment to escapism remains steady.

We tend to hear a lot about the problem of consumerism, which evokes specific images of making insatiable financial purchases and the desire to accumulate more or better stuff. When the topic of consumerism comes up, most of us fall into one of two camps: either we know we're guilty but are overwhelmed at the thought of changing our ways, or we assuage our consciences by thinking of the many people who are doing it worse than we. One way or the other, the inner exploration is generally short-lived.

While material acquisition is a piece of the puzzle, the word "consumerism" shares a root (*consumere*, "to take up" in Latin) with the word "consumption," and it might behoove us to think more in terms of the latter. Rather than fixate on whether or not we are too consumeristic (spoiler alert: we are), which tends to draw our attention exclusively to material objects and shuts down self-reflection rather quickly, we can best identify our personal numbing agents by evaluating our consumption instead. An honest assessment of what we are regularly consuming could point to the unnecessary accumulation of goods, but it could also indicate patterns like excessive media intake or fast-food binges, neither of which leave much of a trail.

None of us is immune to this temptation. Our family has a friend who is a man of strong and unique moral conviction. He doesn't drive a car because of the harmful emissions and its dependence on oil, almost all of the food he eats is either home-grown or retrieved from dumpsters, and all of his clothing was unearthed from some donation bin or another. He has chosen to revolve his life around making socially and environmentally responsible choices, and we respect him for it.

One day this friend and I were in my kitchen, where he was attempting to show me how to make homemade sauerkraut. (I was ready to just go and buy a jar of Bubbies.) He reflected on the recent workshop he had attended to discuss sustainable farming and nonviolent consumption. Unsurprisingly, these kinds of events tend to draw individuals with similar lifestyles to his — people who intentionally order their life to avoid materialism. But, my friend mused, he and his compatriots have their own consumption problem: Even though they live radically simple lives, many are plagued with the consumption of experience. Always looking for the next thing, the next adventure, the next opportunity to travel, they seek to outrun discomfort in search of their own personal form of pleasure. They struggle to put down roots and invest deeply and meaningfully in a community. This is its own form of consumerism, one that is sneakier and more difficult to self-identify.

Yet as Christians, it's not enough to identify what we are consuming and try to pick ourselves up by the bootstraps to simply become more balanced individuals. Our inner lives are only changed when we begin asking why we are overusing these mediums in the first place. What fears, longings, or pains are we trying not to feel when we turn to our own personal drug

> *Instead of turning to God and our fellow man when these aches arise within us, we turn to things that will make the ache go away, at least for a few minutes.*

of choice? This is why I call them numbing agents instead of bad habits. Instead of turning to God and our fellow man when these aches arise within us, we turn to things that will make the ache go away, at least for a few minutes. As a result, the vibrancy of our hearts and minds, and therefore our faith, is at stake.

If you have lived long enough, you have been disillusioned: by life, by people, and, perhaps most of all, by your own self. And even though being wronged by others or suffering difficult circumstances take their toll on our mental and emotional states, nothing stirs the pot of our unrest quite like being a disappointment to oneself. We are generally willing to talk about being wronged by others (though, if the pain is deep enough, not always); but most of us avoid even coming close to talking about the ways we have disappointed ourselves.

When we reach for things to consume, to bring in, in place of addressing our dark and wounded places, we are looking for a way to escape — even if only briefly — the unbearable weight of realizing we aren't who we thought we were. We aren't as strong, we aren't as brave, we aren't as smart, noble, or good. We aren't as successful, we aren't as talented, we aren't as likable, creative, or unique. We are weak, we are relatively insignificant, and we are going to die one day — how'd you like to read that on your next birthday card?

Culturally, we have no good way to discuss these things. Western society has been built around the pursuit of personal kingdoms and impenetrable masks of success, and those who feel the pangs of having fallen short are shamed into silence — unless, of course, after failing you then go on to be wildly successful and publish a memoir about what a pitiful case you once were and how you defeated the odds to become the most successful underwater basket weaver who ever put a toe in the ocean.

But what about those of us who didn't defeat the odds? What about the billions of us who didn't rise from the ashes and achieve everything we ever dreamed and more? Here, it's important to note that the failure to "achieve" can look drastically different from person to person: One man may be devastated to find he wasn't enough to salvage his marriage, while a corporate lawyer might live with the reality that she is the least savvy of the professionals in her firm. A mother may feel the burden of not being able to control her temper, while an injured athlete feels betrayed by the weakness of his own body. Our standards of success and failure may be wildly different, but when it becomes personal, it all looks the same on the inside: dark, lonely, and awfully uncomfortable.

And so, we grasp at the wind; we grasp for the numbing agents that temporarily soothe that internal ache and medicate the despair we feel within. We reach for things, for experiences, for any comfort that will have us. Not all of these are bad, but the danger comes when we use them to replace the hard inner work of opening up our emotions to God and to the people he has put in our lives. No one is claiming that my aforementioned trip to Target was sinful, per se, but what would have happened had I turned the TV on for the kids and spent time in prayer instead? What if I had walked us all to a lonely neighbor's house and offered her companionship out of my own vulnerability? Sometimes it's not a matter of avoiding sin as much as it is about moving toward wholeness.

In the book *You Are What You Love: The Spiritual Power of Habit*, philosophy professor James K. A. Smith likens the rituals of consumerism to a kind of cultural liturgy:

> How do we learn to be consumerists? Not because someone comes along and offers an argument for why stuff will make me happy. ... Rather, I'm covertly conscripted into a way of life because I have been *formed* by cultural practices that are nothing less than secular liturgies. ... These tangible, visceral, repeated practices carry a story about human flourishing that we learn in unconscious ways ... a particular vision of the good life, a rival version of the kingdom, and by our immersion in them we are — albeit unwittingly — being taught what and how to love.[9]

The premise of Smith's book is that our habits don't just reveal what we love, but actually shape what we love; and that as Christians we must have a consistent way to recalibrate our brains away from cultural messages of "the good life" and toward the worship of a God who alone makes us whole. Smith proposes that this

9. James K. A. Smith, *You are What You Love: The Spiritual Power of Habit* (Grand Rapids, MI: Brazos Press, 2016), 45-46, Italics in original.

recalibration is done primarily through the liturgy of Sunday worship, but supportingly through liturgies at home as well — by which he means not a formal church liturgy, but rather the intentional rhythms and routines that create the background against which we learn to live and love. Mindfully choosing to order our lives around examined practices and a specific worldview can anchor our hearts to the primacy of God and serve as a tether when the sheen of consumption would bid us wander. Some people create a personal rule of life or domestic family culture to live by and in, and this is much the same as Smith's liturgies (lowercase "l") of home.

Likewise, the concept could be stretched to fit our purposes here with what I would dare to call a liturgy of weakness. If we orient our lives around rhythms that actively counter the temptation for felt competency and power, we might just find ourselves looking more like Christ and living with more spiritual freedom.

A liturgy of weakness would require that we humble ourselves in imitation of the One in whose footsteps we walk, resisting the shiny distractions of this world to orient our hearts toward an incarnated God and our neighbors who bear his image.

Philippians 2:5–7 exhorts us to have the attitude of Christ Jesus, "who, though he was in the form of God, did not count equality with God a thing to be grasped, but emptied himself, taking the form of a servant, being born in the likeness of men." In order to recalibrate our hearts to look more like Christ, a liturgy of weakness would require that we humble ourselves in imitation of the One in whose footsteps we walk, resisting the shiny distractions of this world to orient our hearts toward an incarnated God and the neighbors who bear his image. What would such a liturgy look like?

Cultivating instead of acquiring

Are all purchases bad? Of course not. Is it wrong to cure a bad mood by visiting a place that brightens your spirits? No. Let us not slip unintentionally into an ill-conceived asceticism here. Pleasure is from God, after all, the One in whose "right hand are pleasures for evermore" (Ps 16:11), and it's certainly possible to enjoy God's good gifts without using them to numb the parts of ourselves we should be offering to others. But as a spiritual practice, a focus on cultivating what God has already given us rather than seeking to acquire more will offer the kind of abundant life that an insatiable consumption never could.

In this practice, cultivating contentment and gratitude in our hearts is critically important, and one way we do that is by practicing generosity with what we have. Rather than wish our homes were updated or larger, we open our current homes to life and love by hosting gatherings and being a place of refuge for the weary. Rather than harbor annoyance about the car that is old and unreliable, we offer to run errands or to pick up friends who need a set of wheels. We counter the lie of scarcity with the discipline of generosity.

A liturgy of weakness begins with the state of the heart, but it doesn't end there. We fight the compulsion toward acquisition by cultivating gratitude, certainly, but also by physically cultivating what we have. We make our homes beautiful by decorating with things stored in the attic or handed down from Grandma instead of picking up the latest home decor item on a Target run (an item that will inevitably end up in a landfill). We plant a garden in the backyard and spend time together in the kitchen cooking instead of making yet another trip to the nearest fast-food joint. We reimagine that old cardigan styled in a new way instead of heading to the mall for the latest sweater rendition.

Learning instead of teaching

This new liturgy of life requires that we do less teaching and more learning, and I'm not talking about learning from the one who has the loudest microphone.

There is nothing innately wrong with listening to, following, and learning from those with big platforms, and often those perspectives can be incredibly beneficial. But to cultivate an intentional position of humility, we must be sure to balance that type of input with the voices of the powerless, the marginalized, and the overlooked. If we hope to be united to the human race to which Jesus forever bound himself, it is imperative that we not neglect the ones whose stories rarely get told, whose cries are seldom heard. If the only perspectives we surround ourselves with are those of the powerful, we will continue to have an imbalanced and inaccurate understanding of the world in which we live. Unfortunately, the perspectives of the powerful are often what we have easiest access to, unless we are intentionally seeking out others.

This translates into our own commitment to learn more than we teach. It is far too easy to espouse a worldview that is the only one we've known without seeking to understand and learn from those who are different, especially those who feel oppressed. To cultivate a life of holy weakness, we must open ourselves up to new perspectives and experiences and be willing to adjust our own opinions accordingly. Exposing ourselves to a narrative that feels foreign does not happen naturally; it demands an effort and openness that will likely make us uncomfortable at times. Yet this is the way of true humility.

Listening instead of talking

This approach to humility begins with making a habit of choosing weakness over power, which takes real effort, because our hearts and minds are not used to giving preference to lowliness. This means, first of all, taking new approaches to old relationships. We're not magically going to do it the right way with people we hardly know if we haven't been working the muscles with those closest to us first. Regular, meaningful conversations with those in your inner circle will never fail to enrich your life, but take stock of the rapport of such conversations. Most of us would benefit from resolving to do more listening than talking in every exchange that we have. As modeled by the traditional Franciscan peace prayer, we as people of peace must, "not so much seek to be consoled as to console, to be understood as to understand, to be loved as to love."

On the other hand, exercising our poverty will sometimes also mean opening our mouths to have the vulnerable conversations we'd rather avoid. Conversations in which we admit our own needs, lacks, and fears, and ask for practical help or simply companionship on our journey can be very difficult, but they are critically important. Many of us are naturally more inclined to listen than to expose our own pain, and remedying this takes a different kind of discipline. We must be willing to take an interpersonal risk with no control over how it will go. In doing so, we dare to take off the protective masks we have worn for so long. We take the risk of being fully known by another with no guarantee they will respond the way we hope.

Resting instead of building

In a world full of admonishments to "hustle" and that you can "sleep when you're dead," taking the Lord's commandment to observe a Sabbath seriously can feel downright subversive. But practicing a liturgy of weakness demands that we slow down and honor the limitations of our bodies, minds, and souls. As Christians, we believe we were lovingly and specifically formed by a Creator who knows our needs, so we can trust that if our Holy Scriptures say we were created to function best with a day of rest every seven, we can trust that our bodies are nurtured by this rhythm.

But it's not just having a twenty-four-hour Sabbath that constitutes rest; it's a lifestyle of choosing to nourish our souls, too. We honor the humanity within us when we say "no" to being stretched thin and "yes" to nurturing our spiritual life, intellect, and interpersonal relationships. We only have so many hours in a week. Each day we are making choices about who and what really matters.

Practicing a liturgy of weakness demands that we slow down and honor the limitations of our bodies, minds, and souls.

Choosing a liturgy of weakness means consciously deciding to make room for rest in our lives. This requires a courageous trust in God that is misunderstood by most; it may even be interpreted as laziness or lack of ambition in certain highly competitive spheres. But nurturing our own inner life will always pay off in ways that tangible achievements cannot. Jesus asks us, "For what will it profit a man, if he gains the whole world and forfeits his life?" (Mt 16:26). In a countercultural liturgy, we step out of the rat race — away from the voices that say we will never succeed by resting — and tend gently to the care of our souls.

I reviewed my packing list for the third time, perplexed by the fastidious departure from my normally laid-back personality. There were no consequences if I forgot something, I reminded myself. A month-long visit in the United States would provide more than enough opportunity to replenish anything I might accidentally leave behind in our Javanese home. Still, I checked and rechecked our packed suitcases, agitatedly picking my cuticles as I made mental note of how outdated my wardrobe looked after being overseas for just a year. The first stop would be my parents' house, and I had already told my mother and sister that shopping and a haircut needed an early place on the itinerary.

Our room was so tiny that the suitcase I packed was splayed open on the bed — there wasn't enough space on the tile floor for it if my husband or I hoped to be able to walk through the doorway. I glanced uneasily down at the spot by the door where the *tokek* (large lizard) had left a puddle of urine a few days before. The forearm-sized amphibian had been scurrying in and out of our bathroom window for weeks, taunting me with the foreboding idea that it would eventually make its way further into the house. They are not vicious creatures, and generally try to avoid humans, but every animal must have a means of defense; theirs is a locked jaw. Once a *tokek* bites down, they can't let go.

"Sounds like something out of a horror movie!" my mom had shuddered over the phone when I'd told her about our houseguest.

I remembered the smell of the reptile's urine. My stomach lurched.

Toothbrush, check. Face wash, check. I zipped up the last of the bags and Eric pulled our oversized shared suitcase out the front door into the hot morning sun, where our ride to the airport awaited. Two days of travel later and I was in my family's arms, only mildly embarrassed by their gigantic signs and giddy display at baggage claim.

For the next four weeks we bounced from family to friends, to the missions' conference that had brought us home in the first place. I bought new clothes, refreshed my hairstyle, and even applied my sister's bottle of self-tanning solution — living in the tropics doesn't equal bronzed skin when you're in a hub of modest Muslim culture. Quickly and carefully, I crafted my appearance to tell a story of a thriving young woman living her dream in an impoverished neighborhood on the other side of the world.

It was a lie, of course; that's not who I was at all. In reality I was disillusioned — with missionary work, yes, but more precisely with myself. My lack of gumption devastated me, and I had spent the better part of our first year overseas in a nominal depression. But what good would it do for anyone to know that? I loathed the fact that I had been trained to give my personal testimony in sixty seconds or less but didn't have the least idea how to alleviate the harrowing effects of poverty in my local context, or even how to find indigenous partners who did. I had visited an orphanage once like some kind of benevolent (or worse, curious) tourist and never went back. Most nights I hid away on our futon watching movies on a laptop, numbing every disappointment that tried to make waves in my brain. The identity I'd clung to was fraying at the seams. How could I say that to Aunt Ruth or the impeccably styled Seattle church-planting mother of three? I couldn't.

Instead, I could say, "Yes, we're getting pretty conversational in *bahasa Indonesia!*" and I could tell anecdotes of life with squatty potties and bucket baths, throwing in the tidbit about our house having beautiful stained-glass windows lest anyone feel too aghast. I could deflect the life crisis that I didn't want to be going through anyway. I could keep saying the things we all wanted to hear.

The ache was too risky to reveal, I decided; I couldn't control it. I couldn't control what would happen if I opened my mouth and let the real truth slither out, which would betray me, so I would make my body and my mouth cooperate to hide my weakness.

Reach for one more piece of jewelry. Reach for the new pair of jeans. Reach to put on a story that isn't yours.

Once you bite down, you can't let go.

Chapter Three

THE INVITATION OF THE INCARNATION

W e were to become parents. Four friends and teammates surrounded us, hot tea set before each of our already sweaty bodies. (The humidity of the Indonesian tropics is only mildly kinder at 9:00 a.m. than at noon.) My husband and I had been in a rush that morning and hadn't undertaken our daily ritual of checking email for any word from Uganda before hopping on our motorcycle to make it in time for the meeting. So, now our friends held their breath with me as Eric, heart pounding, nearly audible, read aloud the words on the screen: "Your court date has been confirmed for December 2. You may go ahead and book your flight to come meet your son."

Someone clicked a camera just in time to catch my husband's fist shoot up in the air and my hands fly over my trembling mouth.

Eric and I had delayed growing our family until after getting settled on the mission field in an attempt to avoid biting off two major life changes simultaneously. Once the time came, we prayed over the choice of trying to conceive or pursuing adoption first. We were young and naïve, but well-meaning and sincere, and the burden of millions of parentless children weighed on our hearts. Adoption it would be.

We initially assumed our child would come from a Southeast Asian country, but when those doors remained sealed shut, I contacted a college friend at a small Christian adoption agency in Texas who confirmed we would be good candidates for their new Uganda program.

Fifteen months later — just weeks after that fated email came — I held my first child for the first time, never, as storyteller Brian Andreas once wrote, to be untouched by him again.

Choosing to adopt sounds like an altruistic endeavor, but the fact is, as with anything, one's motivators are often mixed. As we waded through the paperwork process, I began to feel more acutely the fallen state of my missionary dreams. My team had been trained for two things and two things only: evangelism and discipleship. I knew I wasn't gifted in evangelism, and my commitment to discipleship manifested as long, slow relationships — a far cry from the fast-paced model pushed by our particular vein of church-planting missions. I was trying to shove my square self into an unaccommodating round hole, and it was sucking the life out of me.

I knew my passions lay in applying the Gospel to social constructs, but I couldn't figure out how to do that and was frustrated by the lack of a supportive structure to try. I wanted to see the kingdom of God come to prioritize the poor, the marginalized, and the oppressed, but I was sitting through hours of language school and strategy meetings instead.

No one was stopping me from any pursuit, but no one was joining me either, and I quickly realized that my convictions and passions alone were not enough to materialize social change. I was no leader: I was inhibited, shy, and undeniably a little lazy. Worst of all, I felt like a hypocrite. I espoused the importance of elevating the poor and the orphan, but was completely overwhelmed by how to take initiative on my own and so actually did very little.

The longer the months churned on unremarkably, the more I fixed my eyes on adoption to be the thing to save me from my disillusionment and fear of meaninglessness. I wanted to change the world but felt I was failing. And rather than learn to lean in to that smallness, I hungrily ran to the next promise of strength and success. Weakness couldn't possibly have anything to teach me. If, as it was turning out, I wasn't shaping up to be the next famous missionary, I could prove my spiritual mettle through motherhood instead.

Our first child wasn't even home yet and already I began planning the future adoptions of the second, third, and fourth. In my spare time I scanned postings of waiting children with special needs, imagining a home teeming with "the least of these" that Jesus called us to. They would be loved and cared for; I would be fulfilled. How lucky everyone would be to have me: the orphans, the church, my husband — even God himself.

———————

The Christian call to both service and humility is a tricky one, for loving and serving others can all too easily result in an inflated sense of our own importance. There is something dangerous about feeling needed without having to recognize one's own need in return. Even good intentions can be laced with pride and a subtle thirst for power.

The oft-quoted Scripture on the subject of weakness, 2 Corinthians 12:9–10, tells us that the Lord says, "My grace is sufficient for you, for my power is made perfect in weakness." Paul's response to this is, "I will all the more gladly boast of my weaknesses, that the power of Christ may rest upon me … for when I am weak, then I am strong."

> *The Christian call to both service and humility is a tricky one, for loving and serving others can all too easily result in an inflated sense of our own importance.*

How beautiful an invitation it is to offer our weakness to the Lord, that he may make us perfect and complete. This verse is surely popular because it speaks so hopefully to the places in the human heart that, deep down, know we will always fall short.

But if we are not careful, we can misunderstand this passage as proving that our weakness is something to fix, to fill, to remedy as quickly as possible, rather than as a gift we are given to create longing for God from within. It is tempting to skip over the holiness of weakness here and barrel ahead to the anticipation of God ridding us of it. We still hope that God making up what we lack means ultimately things will work out in our favor or, at the least, in a way that avoids embarrassment.

The power of Christ is a real and true aspect of his person, but Paul was well acquainted with the weakness Christ bore as well. Jesus "did not count equality with God a thing to be grasped, but emptied himself, taking the form of a servant, being born in the likeness of men" (Phil 2:6–7). Paul understood the dichotomy of the strength and weakness of Christ.

We, however, tend to focus only on the power of God. We talk about God as reigning on a throne, and we speak of God's victory, at least in part, to form a narrative in which we also are the victors. We read the Bible and see God become human in order to make right all wrongs and trample the head of the serpent. We focus on God's triumphant qualities and therefore, by extension, assign these qualities to ourselves as Christians. And all of this is true, of course. But it is far from the complete truth.

"The Word became flesh and dwelt among us" (Jn 1:14). How many times have we heard this verse from the opening of the Gospel of John? For many of us the answer is, at least every Christmas. But have we stopped to consider — really, truly, prayerfully, contemplatively — what it means that the uncreated God became destructible flesh?

The idea is so appalling to the human mind that a series of heresies rose up against it in the early centuries of the Church. In fact, the history of the early Church is peppered with Christological heresies, attacking either Jesus' full humanity or divinity. Docetism taught that Christ only appeared to have a human body. Other Gnostics believed that the spirit of Christ temporarily inhabited the body of Jesus. All of these beliefs stemmed from the assumption that the physical world is bad and therefore

God could not become one with it. The First Council of Nicaea settled the question for Christians in A.D. 325, proclaiming that Jesus Christ was fully God and fully man — as distressing to the finite brain as that might be.

But for many of us today, the fact that the man Jesus is *homoousios*, of the same essence as God, is simply a rote tenant of a faith we assent to. We do not look upon it as a universal mystery meant to take our breath away. It is not enough to be awed by the fact that the Maker of the universe became cells in an unwed girl's body. It is not enough to imagine the King of kings being pushed out of a bloody birth canal. It is not enough to assent that the one who holds everything together (cf. Col 1:17) had to have his feces wiped off his backside. As miraculous and mysterious as it is that God took on human form, the implications of the Incarnation run much, much deeper than we realize.

In his treasure of a book, *Poverty of Spirit*, German theologian Johannes Baptist Metz examines the three temptations of Christ in the desert in Matthew 4 as assaults of Satan against the humanity of Jesus. We recall that after his forty-day fast the devil tempted Jesus to use his divinity to obtain food, security, and power. Jesus managed to resist each of these temptations — even in his weakened state — thereby retaining the integrity of his Incarnation. Satan's desire, Metz writes, was "to make Jesus strong, for what the devil really fears is the powerlessness of God in the humanity Christ has assumed."[10]

This sounds pretty counter to the line of thinking we Christians are comfortable with. We are accustomed to crediting the power of God for the defeat of the enemy. So, which is it? Is the devil defeated by God's power, or by God's voluntary powerlessness? Metz continues, "Satan's temptation is ... an enticement to strength, security, and spiritual abundance; for these things will

---

10. Johannes Baptist Metz, *Poverty of Spirit* (Mahwah, NJ: Paulist Press, 1998), 10.

obstruct God's saving approach to humanity in the dark robes of frailty and weakness."[11]

The Incarnation is potent only because Jesus totally embraced the poverty of the human person. Had he used divine might to excuse himself from the painful realities that you and I face in our lifetimes, he could never fully have entered the human experience. The relinquishment of his rights and power was the only thing that could unite him to us in a way that carried any real meaning.

His refusal to bow to Satan (both literally and figuratively) meant more than mere defeat of an enemy who is laughably far from being an equal opponent in the first place. His triumph over Satan in the wilderness was not that he proved himself more powerful; Jesus' victory was that when his divinity could have spared him, he chose to remain poor. In making that choice, he planted his feet firmly on the side of "foolish" love, and followed the precedent straight to the cross.

For what but love could propel God to bind God's self to the human race in such a pitiful way? What else could have motivated God to shed the glories of divinity and don a cloak of the humiliating constraints, limitations, and sufferings of mankind? It was for love, and only love, that God took on our humanity — love for us, yes, but also God's desire for our love in return.

Could we have loved God in the same way if he had not walked this earth as vulnerable as we? Could we have the same capacity for overwhelming devotion if God had not subjected himself to loneliness, grief, hunger, thirst, fatigue, abandonment, betrayal, and longing? Or even if God had not experienced, as my children remind me, human happiness and friendship? In Christ's poverty he proved himself a companion. In his frailty he earned our trust.

Oscar Romero was relatively unsympathetic to the social

---

11. Ibid.

justice movement in El Salvador when he was appointed archbishop in 1977. A kind but predictable man, he was known to
be critical of the progressive stream of clergy who outspokenly
sided with poor farmers seeking land reform during that nation's civil war. But three weeks into his appointment, Romero's
friend and fellow priest Fr. Rutilio Grande was murdered along
with two parishioners — one just a child. Shocked and grieved,
Archbishop Romero went to the little country parish to view
the bodies and comfort his flock. Walking through the crowd
of oppressed and terrified peasants, Romero understood, literally
overnight, that God demanded action of him. No longer could
he remain silent about violence and injustice, protecting himself
and keeping a proverbial peace with a corrupt government while
his vulnerable people were slaughtered — or while the desperate retaliated. He understood that to minister to these people he
must place himself beside them, and he understood that it would
likely cost him his life.

For three years, Oscar Romero preached nonviolence and
justice for the poor, until he was gunned down while saying Mass
on March 24, 1980. With a single bullet to the chest, his blood
splattered onto the holy bread on the altar. The body of Christ,
broken for all.

Can there be a better picture of Christ's incarnation than
this? Rather than distance himself from the absolute mess around
him or use his position of power to protect himself at all costs,
Romero committed fully to his fellow man. He chose poverty
over power, knowing it would kill him, but also knowing that
death is not the end.

Romero's life is a shining example of what the Catholic
Church calls solidarity. The *Compendium of the Social Doctrine of
the Church* explains that the concept "highlights ... the intrinsic
social nature of the human person, the equality of all in dignity
and rights and the common path of individuals and peoples to-

wards an ever more committed unity."[12] Simply put, solidarity means we belong to one another, so we'd better act like it.

The *Compendium* goes on to describe Jesus as the "apex" of solidarity, one "who takes on the infirmities of his people, walks with them, saves them and makes them one. In him and thanks to him, life in society too, despite all its contradictions and

> *Simply put, solidarity means we belong to one another, so we'd better act like it.*

ambiguities, can be rediscovered as a place of life and hope … because it is an invitation to ever higher and more involved forms of sharing."[13]

Perhaps sharing is the operative word here; it is certainly not one used much in Christian dialogue, at least not past the prima-ry-colored classrooms we shuffle our kids into. It's an underused and underrated word for us grown-ups, one we may even be uncomfortable with if we're honest with ourselves. And yet the revolution of Jesus could very well be summed up in such a word. The exhortation to share material goods is there, absolutely, but much more radical is the call to the sharing of power, which is what the *Compendium* is referring to in this society of hope. In Jesus' economy, might and privilege are laid down at the feet of the weak and disenfranchised. Then and only then can both par-ties rise as brothers.

The words Metz uses to describe the ways Satan tried to woo Jesus — words like "strength," "security," and "spiritual abun-dance" — sure do go down easy. So attractive are they to the wayward human heart that many inspirational speakers, pastors, ministries, and churches have gained massive followings (and, let's

---

12. Pontifical Council for Justice and Peace, *Compendium of the Social Doctrine of the Church*, Part VI "The Principle of Solidarity" (Vatican City: Libreria Editrice Vaticana, 2004), 192.
13. Ibid., 196.

be honest, a whole lot of cash) by telling God's people that they are entitled to such things. A Catholic theology of suffering may spare some of us from going down that erroneous road, but the fact of the temptation remains. Mistaking him for a heavenly Santa Claus, it is all too easy to assign an agenda of our own advancement to the will of God.

But maybe we are too enlightened for such bad theology. Perhaps we would never be duped by the "prosperity gospel" or those who profit from it. Good for us; our relationship with God will be deeper for it. But if we are honest, most of us still struggle to fully welcome into our own lives the descriptors we see in the Gospels. For when we search the teachings of the God-Man alive on earth, the words we find take a notably unglamorous and uncomfortable turn: "poor in spirit," "meek," "last." We have spent decades crafting our very existence around strength and success, yet the upside-down kingdom blatantly refuses to play by the rules of the game we know best.

While every internal and external message we receive is telling us to fight for esteem, the example of our incarnated Lord quietly bids us to see the wisdom in his weakness. We must choose between power and solidarity. We simply can't have both and live at peace with a God who turned from every heavenly advantage to gaze evenly into our eyes.

We drove home under a black sky, rain pelting the windshield and him in a deep sleep breathing to the rhythm in the back seat. Thanksgiving at my parents' house had been another battle of wills, Eric and I still mystified by this beautiful boy we had loved for nearly two years. We no longer lived as expats, but navigating this untraditional parenthood back in the States felt every bit as much like wandering in a foreign land.

Motherhood, it was turning out, would not be my crowning glory any more than missions had been. As we drove the full day's journey home, I couldn't hide my disappointment at another holiday survived by the skin of our teeth. Early childhood trauma complicates family life. Strategies that helped other kids' behavior triggered fight-or-flight responses from ours. We were curating an impressively long list of things that didn't work in making him feel calm and safe, but were as hard-pressed as ever to come up with anything that did.

Pain within the family is unlike any outside it — it is overly personal, somehow a reflection of failure of our deepest selves. My husband had his own demons, and I had mine, but we both bent under the shame of failing at something so very important. Our child had been through enough in his short life; he was just a tiny boy acting out of his own fear and grief. He deserved better than this.

Why can't I do this right? My voice broke in the dark.

I had prepared so extensively. I had read all the right parenting books, both adoption and traditional. I had attended church seminars on parenting. I had a college degree in family studies for crying out loud. All around me, my peers were becoming parents and mostly doing okay at it. Sure, everyone agreed that it was difficult, but no one else seemed to be hanging on by the thread we were white-knuckling. There had never been anything in my life I had been so determined to succeed at as mothering, and there had never been anything I had felt I'd bombed so grievously.

Expectations ruin us, yet who can begin any journey completely devoid of them? The overwhelming majority of parenting advice I took in, either through the pages of books or seated in a conference room, convinced me that raising a child is all about authority: the more you lovingly exert, the more the child complies. Simple. Straightforward. Bing, bang, boom: a formula for a happy family. Unfortunately, for my family it had been a formula for disaster.

Eric pulled the car into the driveway late that holiday weekend and the next morning found me, laptop out, registering us for a nine-week training course for adoptive and foster parents.

Empowered to Connect was a ministry of a large Bible church half an hour from our home. With curriculum formed by Dr. Karyn Purvis and her team at Texas Christian University, the training was grounded in the latest research on early childhood trauma. We walked into the room that first Thursday night with the weight of exhaustion and self-loathing heavy on our shoulders. Halfheartedly picking at the bowl of complimentary trail mix before us, I scanned the room, evaluating whether any parent there looked as hopeless as I felt. Some did.

I thought that to be a good parent I had to be in control. I thought if I made enough rules, enough schedules, enough boundaries — coupled with a heaping dose of affection, of course — then my child would thrive and my home would be happy. I wanted to do it for him, for us, for the parts and for the whole. I had envisioned an ideal family life, and I just knew that if I did everything right, we could have it. Struggles would be there, of course, but they wouldn't be too painful or too much. They would feel, as would it all, manageable. But it was not to be.

I didn't realize the depth of the wounds I had been living with until I sat around that circular table every Thursday night that spring. I had been unaware of the power I had been grasping for, the right to control I had deceived myself into assuming I deserved. I was surprised to find myself thinking about my past island life and wondering what my motivations had been during my attempt to be a missionary. How very powerful I had wanted to be, under the guise of altruism and service; how very needed. The similarities between my past and present were too blatant to ignore.

The parent training was potent — at times, uncomfortably so. Years before, when I first read the story of the scales falling from Saint Paul's eyes (cf. Acts 9:18), I never imagined that it hurt. But now I knew the pain that comes from such a necessary shedding. All this time I had been butting my head against the wall of an imaginary family life, one in which my son's behavior and my own unflappable knowledge all served to make me look good in front of others. Now I saw myself in the truth of my ugly arrogance and entitlement. I saw all the ways I had made it about me and not about my child, and by the grace of God I somehow found the good sense to repent and beg for mercy.

"Stop clinging to power as a solution," the Empowered to Connect instructors told a room full of wet-faced parents week after week. "Be with your child in their need. Connection is greater than control." It wasn't a relinquishment of action; connection will always accomplish what control cannot. This is the very message Jesus embodied on earth.

It was at that table, surrounded by two dozen broken souls, that I first realized the only way to be a good parent was to choose the way of the Incarnation. And it was on that journey, too, that I finally realized the only way to be a Christian was to be an incarnational one.

Chapter Four

THE INVITATION
OF THE PASSION

I couldn't breathe.

My palms reached for the wall behind me and, finding it, guided my unsteady body down to the carpet. I had been crying again, chest heaving, brain spinning, body working in overdrive to not break down. That was what it had come to, after all. That was the goal of every day: just make it through, just don't break down, just balance the universe one more time. This time I couldn't.

I had managed to get the kids into the car before my nervous system short-circuited; a mother can't stop being a mother, even on the verge of a panic attack. The cries of the freshly minted four-year-old and the baby I'd brought into the world just months before pounded between my ears, but they were strapped safely into their car seats by the time I realized I was gasping desperately for air.

Where was this God I had given my life to? Where was my "very present help in time of need"? As I sat splayed out on the carpet, wondering what was happening to me and whether I was going insane, was God there, playing some twisted game of hide-and-seek? Or was Jesus as gone as he felt?

It had been more than a year since we had completely changed our approach to parenting, a year that brought the conception and birth of our first biological child as well. Inviting Jesus' Incarnation into our home and our parenting had done a powerful number on my heart, but trauma is not so easily undone. My family still suffered every day, and so did I.

And nothing in my theology had prepared me for it.

He took it too far.

In the Incarnation, God has proved the lengths to which he is willing to go to show us he knows and understands our plight. In the pages of the Gospels, we watch the uncreated God experience physical limitations, painful relationships, public criticism, loneliness, temptation, grief, and more. Jesus' sacrifice is staggering; his commitment to solidarity is almost unbelievable to the human heart. "Stop," we say, "that's enough now." We see where the story is headed and our insides groan in discomfort. "God can't die," we shiver. It's like a horror movie we can't look away from.

But he didn't stop; he wouldn't. He stumbled his way to Golgotha, heartbreak in his eyes, but something else, too: a determined commitment to know us in all our wretchedness and agony — that is, to know us fully.

In the Old Testament, the Hebrew word *yada* means "know," and if you spent your teen years in a youth group like I did, you might have passed a few guffaws and side winks over verses like, "Adam knew Eve" (Gn 4:1). The word does not literally mean the act of sexual intercourse, but it can be used interchangeably because what it does mean is the deepest level of intimacy imaginable. Christians believe that this is what the act of sex is, which is why we value it so highly and reserve it for the confines of a lifetime commitment in marriage. To be in a sexual relationship with another person means to willingly be at our most vulnerable. A healthy sexual encounter is one without a power player. Rather, both

> *In the Incarnation, God has proved the lengths to which he is willing to go to show us he knows and understands our plight.*

parties come together offering their physical and emotional vulnerability to one another in full mutuality. Adam knew Eve — and Eve knew Adam — as they experienced the most profoundly intimate human experience together.

But sex is not the only context wherein *yada* is used. We read in many places that God knows us, such as Psalm 139:1, where we learn that he has searched us and known us. In theory, we believe it. We understand in our heads that he knows us with all the intimacy experienced by a lover, but it is a difficult and awfully intangible message to get across to the human heart. Yet the Incarnation made it tangible: God's love put skin on.

Similarly, when we're in the midst of suffering, it can feel far-fetched to believe that God shares our pain. What does the Divine really know of a broken heart? But Jesus Christ on the cross cannot be denied. God has known us in our weakness and in our suffering. He has known us and has called us his.

For non-Catholics, seeing a crucifix can be uncomfortable. Protestants have been known to declare things like: "He's not on the cross anymore! He is risen!" And it goes without saying that those things are true. But there is something deeper in that discomfort, something akin to fear and an avoidance of pain.

For Catholics, on the other hand, seeing a crucifix can become meaningless. Familiarity can rob us of the meaning of the cross. We replace its profundity with, at best, a glance of acknowledgment and maybe a quick Sign of the Cross over our head and chests. But there is something deeper in that forgetting, something akin to fear and an avoidance of pain. The two responses are more similar than different.

I never really expected to meet Christ on the cross. The expression of Christianity I had been most formed in was much more likely to emphasize the Resurrection than the crucifixion. Other than the part in the evangelism tract about Jesus dying for our sins, there didn't seem to be much to talk about. I had watched the Passion dramatically unfold before me in church plays more times than I could count, but I had never seen past the basic storyline that I knew by heart. Maybe, until you're the one in pain, you never do.

What we miss when we skim over the Passion — or, alternatively, when we reduce it to a kind of legal exchange between a holy God and the problem of sin — is the companionship of Christ in the most horrifying places on earth. Simultaneously bearing excruciating physical suffering, devastating victimization, and a burden that he literally cannot carry, Jesus voluntarily walks the darkest road of human experience toward us who thought we were alone on it.

It is the ones who are suffering — Catholic, Protestant, or non-Christian — who draw near to Christ crucified like moths to a flame. It is the ones who have been shipwrecked and ravaged, the ones who cannot escape from nor ever fully numb their need and their poverty. These ones no longer have the luxury of looking away from a crucifix. They search for their own experience reflected back to them, and in it they see a God who intimately understands, who knows them in the *yada* sense of the word. He is simply magnetic hanging there, that Jesus, and the willing human heart will always be drawn.

Of all people in the world, you would think Christians would have a rich theology of suffering. We are the ones who worship a God who was murdered, after all. Yet although much established doctrine on the subject does, of course, exist, a lack of comprehensive catechesis is a problem, and even the most devout among us can easily fall prey to widespread myths and traps.

In the ninth chapter of the Gospel of John, the beloved disciple gives an account of Jesus healing a blind man. When they come upon him, the disciples ask Jesus whose sin was responsible for the man's affliction — his own or that of his parents? In the twenty-first century, most of us have a theology that has evolved past such an idea of a punitive God who cruelly doles out physical ailments as punishment for sin. We know God better than that, or so we think. Yet we are not without myths of our own: These days we're more likely to be guilty of subtly placing the burden of responsibility on the person afflicted, not accusing them of sin per se, but of making a mistake that could have been avoided — or even should have been.

We do this not to be intentionally spiteful, but because seeing suffering as a natural consequence of what someone has either done or failed to do allows us to hope we might be exempt if we play our cards right. We silently comfort ourselves with accusatory explanations that seek to alleviate our own fears that such devastation could happen to us: *The birth defects are probably because she took antidepressants before pregnancy. He wouldn't have been hit by a drunk driver if he had not been out past midnight. Their child got into drugs because they didn't go to church regularly.* On and on and on we go. We'll make any leap to convince ourselves that we have some control over tragedy, not unlike the people of Jesus' day. Perhaps we haven't evolved so very much at all.

When the disciples ask Jesus this question, he answers, "It was not that this man sinned, or his parents, but that the works of God might be made manifest in him" (Jn 9:3), and then he proceeds to heal the man. Notice that Jesus does not necessarily say that God made this man blind on purpose, nor that God did not do so. There will always be an element of mystery that we are left to wrestle with when faced with suffering; there may always be more questions than answers. Jesus doesn't give an exhaustive apologetic on omnipotence or divine will here. But what he does imply is that where suffering exists, so also can mercy. Where despair exists, there is room for hope to come. Where darkness exists, light will be seen. Where tragedy exists, love speaks all the more loudly. This is how the works of God can be made visible: goodness abounds and the image of God in human beings is revealed just a little more.

It has become commonplace for Christians to refer to suffering as a "test." This never fails to baffle me, and I wonder that believers can manage to remain faithful while laboring under that image, as though the One who is goodness itself should be sitting

on a throne with a red pen, ready to mark us as passing or failing
while watching our pain apathetically. Who would want to de-
vote themselves to a God so ... *mean?* Suffering is an opportunity,
to be sure — a chance to let Our Lord intimately console and
guide us, as well as an occasion to grow and to be sanctified —
but trauma and loss are not pass-or-fail tests administered by God.

Some Christians also believe that suffering in and of itself
makes us holy. This couldn't be further from the truth. Suffering
in itself does not make us holy; it is our response to it that does
the sanctification, and this is easier said than done. Like Jesus, we
are well advised to ask the Father to spare us if possible. In the
Garden of Gethsemane, on the last night of his life, Jesus was in
such distress that Luke tells us "his sweat became like great drops
of blood falling down upon the ground" (Lk 22:44). As God,
Jesus knew the torture and mocking that were soon to come. As
man, he was terrified. With knees in the grass and forehead in the
dirt, he pleaded with the Father, "If you are willing, remove this
chalice from me" (v. 42).

Normally, when we think of the cup of Christ, we think of
the blood of Christ in the Eucharist, poured out for us. Yet Jesus'
prayer in Gethsemane reveals another layer to the image. The cup
he asks his Father to remove from him is the cup of suffering.
This biblical cup of suffering both fascinates and terrifies me, and
I think both are appropriate reactions. That Jesus himself experienced suffering gives validity to his humanity. After all, could he
really have claimed to be man while dodging it completely? But
it is his plea to be spared that makes us believe his solidarity. Even
with skin on, God does not always feel accessible to humankind,
but show us one small floundering of strength in the face of a
coming anguish and our hearts leap within us. *Brother!* We know
that feeling all too well.

This isn't the first we've seen of this cup in the Gospels. Matthew narrates a time when brothers James and John were vying for

positions of prominence in the kingdom of heaven, even letting their mother somewhat awkwardly recommend them for the seats on either side of the Lord. Jesus' response — rather than reprimand them for their arrogance, as they probably deserved — is to ask if they can drink the cup which he must drink (cf. Mt 20:22), insinuating that the cup contains something categorically undesirable. The two disciples say they can, and, indeed, Jesus prophesies that they will, but there is an air of foreboding in the whole exchange.

When we married, Eric and I each brought our own prized possessions to our newfound family. My most notable were a turquoise five-by-seven-foot shag rug that I thought was the epitome of style and an accompanying overweight pug dog that more or less went with it. Luckily for me, Eric is also internally wired to love odd-looking things and was immediately endeared to both, so I knew our marriage would stand the test of time. For his part, Eric came with books: Shelves and shelves of books, many of which I still have not cracked open twelve years later, because I have yet to live through a day rainy enough to call out for Nietzsche. But I digress.

One of these books was the collected poems of Rumi, a Sufi mystic whom I weighed cautiously and not without a little suspicion. It wasn't until after coming home from Indonesia — after the concrete edges of my black-and-white brain had begrudgingly begun to embrace a bit of mystery — that I cracked it open. I was surprised to find a world of gospel from this Muslim poet and remembered what my theologian father had always said: "All truth is God's truth." You would think I might have discovered this by living in Southeast Asia for nearly two years, but it just goes to show you how very non-catholic my worldview was.

I quickly became a fan of Rumi's and latched on to several poems in the book (much to Eric's slightly smug delight), but one of my favorites was "Not a Day on Any Calendar." I was especially drawn to one particular line:

Around the lip of the cup we share, these words:
My Life Is Not Mine

I can't *not* think of Jesus' cup when I read Rumi's words. This cup of suffering is one I drink with every other human being on the planet, if for no other reason than because it is one I share with a God who became human to share it with me. By his voluntary acceptance of this cup, Jesus drinks in solidarity with every kind of suffering there is. And because of his drink, solidarity is extended to me and from me as well. My life is not mine, so with my Lord I will share this cup that others are carrying, too — their pain is mine because their pain is God's.

━━━━━━━

Many of us know someone who has experienced a medically unexplainable healing, whether spontaneously through a time of prayer or between one medical checkup and the next. We would be remiss not to acknowledge that the supernatural permeates the natural and that such divine healings do still occur. And yet, another myth of suffering is that our piety or devotion can make miracles happen. Not many Christians would ever think to use such bold language, but how often do we fall prey to the idea that we can pray or fast our way to healing? "If I just pray harder, longer, better," we tell ourselves. "If I just had more faith." Certainly, Scripture exhorts us to persevere in prayer, but the slope between uniting ourselves to him in faith and insisting on a certain outcome is a slippery one.

I didn't begin sliding down that hill until college, but the effects were strong by the time I entered into marriage and parenting. I assumed that doing God's will meant God would make it easy, that healing in our home would almost be a reward for our faithfulness. I believed that God's will for all people was wholeness — holiness — but I subconsciously assumed my spiritual devotion meant I would get to walk a lighter path.

As the months rolled by and family life continued to feel more like Good Friday than Easter Sunday, I felt my theology begin to unravel. Who was this God who would not snap his fingers and heal? I hardly knew him, and I certainly did not feel *yada*-ed by him. As time went on, it became harder and harder to believe God would move on our behalf; most days I wondered if God even remembered us at all.

The only comfort I had was that Jesus himself had felt this way before.

One of the most agitating lines of Jesus (and he has some doozies) is found in Matthew 27:46: "*Eli, Eli, lama sabach-thani?*" or "My God, my God, why have you forsaken me?" Hanging on the cross, just moments before his death, having been tortured and humiliated for hours, he is desperate for even just a shimmer of consolation from his Father. It doesn't seem like too much to ask, does it? Just a touch of the heart, just a confirmation of God's nearness. But he gets none.

Theologians disagree on whether or not the Father had actually allowed a separation between himself and the Son. I know that this point is not inconsequential when it comes to hammering out important theology, but, call me simple-minded, I'm okay with not knowing. What's important to me is not whether Jesus actually was abandoned, but that he honestly felt abandoned. In his darkest hour — one that makes my own trials pale in comparison — he cried out for God's presence and comfort with the only hope left in him.

And he felt nothing in return.

In solidarity with every person who has ever felt forgotten by God, Jesus Christ hung from the wood that dark Friday afternoon. In solidarity with the child who believes her abuse proves she's not good enough to matter to God, Jesus hung. In solidarity with the man who begs God to keep him from drinking only to pour another glass against the silence, Jesus hung. In solidarity with me weeping alone in my closet where the rest of my family couldn't hear, Jesus hung. And for all those currently in their own darkest hour, praying desperately to the black hole and feeling nothing in return, he hangs there still.

━━━━━━━━━━━━━

I laced my sneakers and pulled up the prayer app on my phone, shouting a goodbye to Eric as I slipped in my earbuds and closed the front door behind me, quickly, before someone might need something and completely thwart my attempt at postpartum self-care. As I had done every Friday that Lent, I scrolled through the app to find the recitation of the Stations of the Cross and, pressing play, embarked on my sluggish jog.

It was April in Texas and already hot. My legs pumped begrudgingly, knees filing complaints against me as I shuffled along, but for once my mind was not much given to the burn of my body.

We adore you O Christ and we bless you, because by your holy cross you have redeemed the world.

I began with him at his condemnation and continued on to behold him carry his cross and then fall for the first time. I thought of how we don't make enough of Jesus' falls on the Via Dolorosa. After all, right there before us is a picture of our lives: the unbearable burdens we have no choice but to carry and all the ways they bring us to our knees. Soon Simon of Cyrene would be called on to help him. Soon Jesus would know what it is to be unable to carry your burden alone. But for now, the Station I had waited for: the fourth, the account of Jesus meeting his mother.

I had been enamored with the idea of having a relationship with Mary for months, but she continued to remain an enigma to the mind of one who for three decades only ever considered her existence at Christmastime. Regardless of my attraction, actually knowing Mary as a mother never felt very likely. But as I ran, the words prayed through this Station became larger than life. My imagination took over as I bathed in the story of a mother witnessing the suffering of her beloved son. The prayer in my ear was one I knew intimately in my own heart: The suffering of a woman's child that she could not take from him, and the suffering of her own heart in response. Our circumstances were wildly different, Mary's and mine, but it didn't matter to me. The tears fell hot and fast. Someone understood.

Jesus was near me in my suffering, and so was his mother, she fully human and grief-stricken as I. In opening ourselves to the weakness of the Incarnation, Eric and I had become softer and more open parents, yes, but better spouses and human beings as well. I wanted that to be enough; I wanted it to stop there.

Yet to know this God–Man fully and be fully changed by him, we have to know him not just in his humanity, but in his deepest suffering, too. For that is his place of most intimate encounter with the world — not in his power and might, but in his weakness and grief. That is where he meets the deepest pain of humankind, and where he invites us to do the same. This is not suffering

> *To know this God-Man fully and be fully changed by him, we have to know him not just in his humanity, but in his deepest suffering, too.*

for the sake of suffering itself, but because our capacity for true love is found only in the lowest place.

For more than three years I had prayed continuously and fervently for our family to be healed. But in one thirty-minute run, I realized that contrary to all my crying, raging, and spiritual bargaining, the truth was, it was better that we hadn't been.

Chapter Five

LONGING AND BELONGING

"Come look at this!" my husband shouted from his office on the other side of the house.

Curiosity piqued, I dried my hands on the nearest dishrag and left the kitchen sink, stepping over the heads of boys sprawled on the floor, and walked down the hall. The website he had pulled up on the computer screen was familiar. It held a list of every location of active Catholic Worker communities in the nation and around the world. We had been drawn to the Catholic Church and her social teaching, and we had checked this website before and found no listing near us. But this time I followed the point of his finger to see the name of our city right there under "Texas."

I tried to match Eric's enthusiasm but found I couldn't muster the hope necessary to do so. We had been isolated and lonely for nearly two years, both because of our unique family needs that limited social engagements and because our faith was currently straddling the Protestant and Catholic worlds. We could no longer ignore the theological disparity we felt in evangelical circles but were definite outsiders in the rigid culture of Catholicism as well.

Not only were we spiritually homeless, but we felt an emotional burden as well. My husband and I were manifesting signs of secondary trauma, and more often than not the anxiety of social situations was enough to keep us home behind locked doors. It's hard to connect meaningfully with others when you can't stick around at a gathering long enough to learn a few names. As well-intentioned as everyone around us had been, our society is simply not set up to accommodate families with extenuating circumstances. Over time, the only solution seemed to be to stop trying.

Somewhere deep within, I was giving up the hope of ever belonging anywhere. "Maybe we'll just be on our own forever. It's not what I wanted, but it's not so bad," I lied to myself. It had been a long few years, and I was too disillusioned to feign real optimism.

"I'm going to email them right now!" His excitement was palpable, and I was trying hard not to quench it — better that one of us held on to hope. "Great!" I agreed. "Sounds good. Let me know when they respond. I'm going to go nurse the baby."

Back in the living room I folded my legs under me in the overstuffed armchair and nestled my infant in tight while the preschooler ran laps around the couch. I wanted to pray, "Please God, let this be a consolation," but when I opened my mouth hot tears dripped in where words should be.

———————

The first time I walked into the Day House, I felt like an outsider. I was too well dressed, too privileged, too educated, too married. But I lingered anyway, awkward as it was, and having a baby in tow always makes finding conversation a bit easier. The Day House was the Catholic Worker house of hospitality my husband had found online, a modest hub welcoming everyone, but with the specific intention of providing a warm place of rest for people experiencing homelessness. Having grown up with two parents whose hearts bled behind them everywhere they went, I was no stranger to such settings. But the perceived aptitude with which I used to serve was now gone; I no longer had the same reserves of energy or certainty to draw from as an offering for others. Here I found myself in the peculiar position of being the one in need, desperately hoping for a seat at the unlikely table of community this group had forged for themselves.

I soon learned this meant I fit right in at the Catholic Worker. This was a small part of a greater movement that began in 1933 through the combined efforts of Dorothy Day and Peter Maurin to put the Church's teachings of mercy and solidarity into action for the benefit of the most downtrodden. The ethos of the Catholic Worker movement is that we are *all* in need and we are *all* able to give, therefore no one serves another without themselves gaining something from him or her.

In fact, this is the distinctive difference between the Day House and every other attempt at the works of mercy I had participated in before it. At the Day House it was difficult for an outsider to distinguish who was indigent or who was in charge: Everyone was invited to participate in the chores of the house and the preparation of the meals, and everyone was invited to make suggestions and provide input. The four young men who made the big decisions and bore the major responsibilities wanted it this way. The intention of the house was to level the playing field, share resources and power, and honor the dignity of all guests without a distinction between "the benevolent" and "the needy," knowing that every human being has the simultaneous capacity to fill both roles.

The first time we were present for dinner, I hesitated to receive any of the food, lest it deprive a hungry guest of a full belly that night. It was quickly explained to us (and I can't say for certain whether words were used or not) that dining together was the most profound act that took place at the Day House. If we, the comparatively wealthy, declined to eat with and beside the poor, we would reinforce the very barriers the group was trying so hard to dismantle. If those who could afford to eat later, in the comfort of our own homes, chose not to partake in the community meal — even with the purest motives — the table no longer became the great equalizer, but yet another reinforcement of divisive socioeconomic lines. The traditional soup-kitchen model tends to keep us in our respective boxes, we came to understand. A community table equalizes all. Miraculously, just as Dorothy Day once wrote, "There was always bread."[14]

Operating out of a place of strength and competency is the default mode for most of us, conditioned as we are to wrestle in

---

14. Dorothy Day, *The Long Loneliness: An Autobiography* (New York: Harper & Row, 1952), 285.

a society that believes to its core in the survival of the fittest. A mirage of power elicits a certain degree of admiration from our fellow man, but it also makes it difficult to truly belong. Power is alienating. Our weakness, on the other hand, links us together. It is a natural bonding agent that builds intimacy between people. Exposing our own weakness can be humiliating, but contrary to our instinctually negative response, that is not necessarily a bad thing. The word "humiliation" comes from the Latin *humilis*, meaning low. Merriam–Webster defines humiliation this way: "to reduce to a lower position in one's own eyes or in others' eyes." While shame or embarrassment can result from humiliation, note that neither is part of its definition. To be made lower in perceived position can even be healthy, if we are willing to look at the truth about ourselves with an open spirit. Unfortunately, we often are not willing to look at this truth, and the result is shame. If, after experiencing the discomfort of being made low, we invite shame in, we will spend the rest of our lives either incapacitated by it or overcompensating for it. Growth and health only come when we reject shame, embrace humility, and have compassion on ourselves, for compassion on ourselves will always lead to compassion for others.

So how do we let humiliation lead to growth, to humility? The tricky part is, it's impossible to live out a revelation of our own inner poverty by simply willing ourselves to do it. Spiritual willpower has its place, we need only look at things like fasting, prayer, and sacrifice to see that, but there is a point where its efficacy ends. Poverty of spirit is that point. Poverty of spirit is the point where you realize that your boot straps will do you no good here. You cannot embrace

> *You cannot embrace your weakness by means of your own strength.*

your weakness by means of your own strength. Neither can this weakness simply be taught: Like all encounters with Christ, we must experience it in order to be transformed by it.

The only way to lay hold of spiritual fruit that cannot come through mental gymnastics is by allowing our weaknesses to lay us low. We must receive our suffering, disappointments, failures, and inadequacies as the invitations that they are: invitations to see our tiny but precious part in the whole of redemptive history. We can choose not to numb our pain but to let it propel us to find solace and companionship by bringing our fragility before God and man. Only through the opening up of our whole, authentic selves — not merely selecting the best parts we want to show the world — can we begin the slow work of getting comfortable with our discomfort.

It is in this honest confrontation with all we lack that we are finally able to recognize the truth of what the Creator spoke about human beings from the very beginning: *We are good*. Note that this is not just *you* or *I*, but *we*, the human race, made in the image and likeness of a very good God. *We* are good, just as he declared us to be in the beginning of time. In all of our failures and struggles and setbacks, he has pronounced us good. In all of our seeking to love and being hurt along the way, he whispers that we are good. We are good because we are God's, and the smallest and most tender places buried inside contain his love. When we learn to accept ourselves in our own weakness, we then begin the long journey of accepting the weakness of others, too.

On this matter, no one speaks with greater potency or authority than Jean Vanier. Vanier is the founder of L'Arche, an international network of communities comprised of people with intellectual disabilities and typically-abled individuals who live alongside them, not as professional caregivers but as friends. Bucking the tradition of group homes for the handicapped (served by a generally good-hearted staff who clock out at the end of their shift), L'Arche is a groundbreaking model of solidarity, a place where, as Vanier says, "The one who is healed and the one who is healing constantly change places."[15] Priest and popular author Henri Nouwen is probably its most famous resident.

Vanier has lived his entire adult life, which is nearing its end, in deep companionship with intellectually disabled friends — proof that he doesn't just talk the talk of human interconnectedness through weakness, but faithfully walks the walk. Through his quiet and humble life experience, Vanier has absorbed profound wisdom on the human condition, particularly as it concerns weakness and strength.

In *Becoming Human*, one of his many excellent books, Vanier writes, "If we deny our weakness … if we want to be powerful and strong always, we deny a part of our being, we live an illusion. To be human is to accept who we are, this mixture of strength and weakness. To be human is to accept and love others just as they are. To be human is to be bonded together, each with our weaknesses and strengths, because we need each other. Weakness, recognized, accepted, and offered, is at the heart of belonging, so it is at the heart of communion with one another."[16]

If we have been broken by life, we can be sure that the breaking is unto greater belonging.

When a Pharisee tried to trick Jesus by asking him to name the greatest commandment, Jesus took the invitation as an opportunity to catechize his listeners: "You shall love the Lord your God with all your heart, and with all your soul, and with all your mind. This is the great and first commandment. And a second is like it, You shall love your neighbor as yourself" (Mt 22:37–39). And then, the icing on top: "On these two commandments depend all the law and the prophets" (v. 40).

---

15. Jean Vanier, *Becoming Human* (Toronto: Anansi Press, 1998), 25.
16. Ibid., 40.

The whole law and the prophets. Every meticulously detailed nook and cranny of our faith hinges on the simple call to love the Lord and love our neighbor. Most of us spend an exorbitant amount of time trying to do the first one well; we know the importance of orienting our lives around the love of God and are quick to read new books, try new disciplines, listen to new worship music, or pray new novenas to propel that devotion forward. But when it comes to the second greatest commandment — that of loving our neighbor as ourselves — well, most of us more or less hope that one shakes out on its own.

Yet, when asked about what our faith hinges on, Jesus couldn't name the first without also naming the second. Clearly, he wants us to take the call of the latter equally as seriously as the former. The Pharisee didn't ask Jesus for the two most important commandments, but they are so closely related that it seems Jesus is saying you simply can't talk about one without talking about the other. "The second is like it," he says. *Like it?* How can anything be like loving God with all our hearts, souls, and minds?

There is a profound truth Jesus is communicating here: The image of God, the *imago Dei*, is so deeply ingrained in the human person that loving your neighbor cannot be differentiated from loving your God. They are two sides of the same coin, as cosmically inseparable as hydrogen and the sun.

> *The imago Dei is so deeply ingrained in the human person that loving your neighbor cannot be differentiated from loving your God.*

"To love another person is to see the face of God," wrote Victor Hugo in the now-famous line from *Les Misérables*. This is a profound and moving idea, but, no offense to Hugo, it's not an original one.

In the Gospel of Matthew, Jesus makes the bold claim that

we will face eternal judgment based not on our piety or religious scruples, but on how we treated one another. Those who inherit the kingdom, he explains, will do so because, "I was hungry and you gave me food, I was thirsty and you gave me drink, I was a stranger and you welcomed me, I was naked and you clothed me, I was sick and you visited me, I was in prison and you came to me" (Mt 25:35–36).

The righteous whom he will reward will have no recollection of doing such things for him and will ask what on earth he is talking about. So, he clarifies, "Truly, I say to you, as you did it to one of the least of these my brethren, you did it to me" (v. 40). Once again, we witness Jesus trying to give us eyes to see the divine image in one another. Once again, he seems to tell us: If you want to be closer to God, all you need do is move closer in to your neighbor.

But when we endeavor to live this teaching, sooner or later we hit an ugly and inconvenient snag: our pride. We can attempt to live the works of mercy all day long, but until we allow ourselves to be broken open, weaknesses exposed, we will never fully stand in the place of solidarity we long for. Without being confronted by our own inner poverty and smallness, we can never make sense of the poverty of another. Without weakness, we are in danger of living a life of hollow benevolence without truly meeting Christ in the face of the other; we will condemn ourselves to staying in the shallow end of the pool of God's love.

Yet if we can embrace our own humiliations, that can be the conduit that ushers us into the communion with others that God so desires for his people. When we befriend our own shadows and stop denying their existence, we will be surprised by how readily we see ourselves in the plight of our neighbors. As Jesus tells us, "Unless a grain of wheat falls into the earth and dies, it remains alone; but if it dies, it bears much fruit" (Jn 12:24). If we dare to let our pride die, we will be astonished by what grows.

For me, that cycle of death and growth has been most pronounced through parenting. I had fantasized my entire life about how natural and fulfilling it would be to have children, but the actual experience has confirmed not my strengths, but my staggering inadequacies instead. This shock was particularly brutal in the beginning. (I have become far less surprised by my maternal shortcomings over the course of time and babies.) When I found myself in the pit of despair, clearly not doing enough for what marriage and family required of me, I was taken aback to find Jesus Christ sitting down there in the muck, holding my hand. If I thought I had loved him before, it didn't hold a candle to the gut-wrenching worship of discovering him beside me in my most humiliating places. It turns out, that was always where he'd been.

The grain of my pride had fallen to the earth and died, but it wasn't the end of the story. The fruit of such a death has been to see myself rightly and, in doing so, to gain the ability to see others in compassion and not judgment. After the adoption of our son and only a few months of living under extreme stress, tight finances, and sleep deprivation, the rope of my mental health quickly began fraying at the edges. I came to empathize with the parents I had once cast judgment upon, even those who had failed their children terribly. No person is a soulless monster, I realized; we simply can't keep bending without a breaking point, and there are mothers and fathers out there who carry more burdens than I can even begin to fathom.

Eric and I were barely hanging on with the luxury of four supportive parents, healthy friends who listened and tried to understand, and the benefit of higher education to inform us. Recognizing how much I struggled to control my temper under unprecedented life stress — even with those assets — completely silenced my criticisms of other parents' failures. For example, now I see that abuse is something to be grieved deeply, not just for the child, but for the parent as well. Neither should have to live with those kinds of demons. Energy I once spent on judgment can now go toward prevention, through reaching out to at-risk parents in solidarity and supporting public policies that strengthen all families.

Whatever our circumstances are, when we begin to respond to our brokenness with openness, we can take on new perspectives that better reflect the love and compassion of God toward others. In addition, being open and vulnerable about our struggles with others lends them a new perspective through which to see, too. For instance, when I confide to a friend who isn't a parent that my own temper has scared me in motherhood, she might walk away with more compassion for the angry mom she notices in Walmart. Likewise, when a divorced friend tearfully explains how excruciating the dissolution of his marriage was, I, who have never experienced that degree of marital strain, am less likely to pass judgment the next time someone I know announces a separation. Listening to the childhood memories of someone who spent the previous night in a jail cell will undoubtedly change the way you see the incarcerated. The more exposure we get to the plight of our fellow humans, the harder it becomes to villainize them.

Empathy changes us; it changes how we see the world, and it changes how likely we are to make an "other" out of our neighbor. This is one reason why embracing weakness matters — and why choosing to be honest about it can change more than just your own perspective. When you choose not to be vulnerable about your own weakness, you deny someone else the perspective for compassion they might have carried back into the world. And sometimes that someone is the person in the mirror.

I fastened the strap of the bright red, 1920s-style shoe around my ankle, unable to remember the last time I had worn heels. But today was a celebration. Tina barreled into my bedroom with her trademark energy excess and a long braid. I'd never seen her hair styled that way before, and the gesture of elegance for the special occasion moved me. It also ensured that her neck tattoo would be on full display. I smiled.

"You ready? We gotta go!" she urged, her excitement disguised as impatience, but I knew better. I followed her out of the bedroom, picking up the little baptismal gown on my way. In our kitchen, people congregated eagerly, putting finishing touches on the spread of food that would be devoured in an hour. Cathy may have been homeless, but I'd take her peanut butter chocolate cake over almost any other dessert in the world. Someone was assigning seats in the caravan to the church, and I found my four-year-old in the buzz. In the ten minutes since I had gotten him dressed, there had already appeared a smudge of something on his little blue pinstripe blazer, and I licked my finger to scrub it off as we all shuffled out the door.

Vans that doubled as homes trailed behind as we led the pack, bodies folded into our reliable SUV like a circus-clown car. The baby shrieked gleefully, an extrovert to the core at six months old, and the preschooler sang along with his godfather at the top of his lungs.

We had requested a private baptism — partly in light of our older son's anxiety, but also partly because we knew we'd be bringing a crowd. Walking through the church doors, I felt my heart drop just a little: Some of the Day House friends we'd invited hadn't come, their affection for our two children not enough to surpass a lifetime of hurt by Christians. "Oh yeah, I know that church," sixty-year-old Johnny had told me when I invited him days before. "They hosted a big event for us a year or two ago. They all wore T-shirts that said, 'Party with the Poor.'"

My cheeks had flushed and burned hot. Eric and I had been confirmed into the Catholic Church only a few months prior, and a large part of the attraction had been the rich history of social teaching. Clearly, this teaching still had a lot of trickling down to do. Needless to say, Johnny didn't show up for the baptism.

But plenty of others did. I held the baby back from his relentless mission of splashing in the baptismal font, scanning the small crowd of our loved ones. My Baptist parents were there in the front row, gamely chatting with our boys' godparents and embracing this whole foreign ritual as our choice to make for our children and not their own. My heart swelled with gratitude at the two-day road trip it had taken for them to be there. They wouldn't have missed it.

Sixty-year-old women who lived on the streets gathered around. College students snapped photographs to gift us later. Single godparents wrangled our kids. The Indian priest gave us instructions I struggled to understand, so thick was his accent, even to my traveled ears. Two of my son's friends, children adopted from Haiti by some of our fellow parishioners, swung their feet from the pew. We could hardly have compiled a more universal group if we had tried. Catholic indeed.

The Rite of Baptism began, with all its play to the senses through water, candles, oil, and recitation. The community around us had literally held our family together for the past six months: They had rallied in prayer after my panic attack, they had provided respite care for our children, they had seen me cry during Lectio Divina, they had sped to my parked car in moments of crisis. Our family had offered this motley crew our weary, wounded hearts, and they had cupped them in dirty, tender hands.

The rainbowed voices of unlikely saints rang through my ears — eager promises to love and uphold us as we walked the narrow way of Christ with our children, promises they had already proven themselves good for. One year ago, we had never felt so alone. Now this.

In the orphanage from which we adopted our oldest son, there was a giant mural on one wall that read, "God puts the lonely in families," referencing Psalm 68:7 and serving as an optimistic prophecy over the infants and toddlers who populated the home. We had taken our first family picture against that wall, the three of us — Eric and I full of gratitude (and maybe a bit of pride) over the chance to be a family for the lonely, a quizzical but contented expression on our little boy's face. It was a profound picture, but what we assumed would be the end of the story was only the beginning. Eventually, it would be our turn for need. Eventually, we would be the lonely whom God promised to set in family. And, eventually, we would learn that perhaps this is the great love story of the human race — that sooner or later we all have the chance to be family for another.

Chapter Six

TRANSFORMATION AT HOME

M y point having been made, I leaned back against my chair in smug triumph. Case closed, argument won. Clearly, Eric just needed to be more like me. If he could approach the situation with my own frame of mind, everything would be easier. Better. Over.

"You're being a bully again," my husband sighed, taking off his glasses to rub the space between his eyes. "You're not trying to understand my perspective at all."

Some selective retorts shot through my brain, but I held my tongue and rolled my eyes instead. Passive aggression has always been my forte, although Eric wasn't wrong about the bullying, either. I get hotheaded when I fear being controlled. "That fiery Irish temper," he would describe it near adoringly on better days, inexplicably endeared to the opposite of his more contemplative nature. But over the years it has become a guest less welcome in the heat of the moment.

We were having the same old fight we'd been having for years, responding the same way we always had: I, feeling angry and resentful; he, feeling maligned and dismissed.

Relational patterns are as fixed as markings in sidewalk cement, our initials inside a heart left out to dry in the heat of the day. What does it take to disrupt them? They don't scrub off; they won't be painted over. Maybe the only way forward is to take a jackhammer to the whole thing, or blow it to smithereens. Maybe we'll only find redemption in the rubble.

Our pain will not be our undoing.

Or, perhaps better said, our pain *will* be our undoing, but not our ending. For we only need look at the earth around us to see that God has ordained darkness as the way to life abundant: winter to spring, caterpillar to butterfly, sand to pearl. Jesus taught us,

"Unless a grain of wheat falls into the earth and dies, it remains alone; but if it dies, it bears much fruit (Jn 12:24).

All life around us first goes through the appearance of death, so why should we be any different? We are part of a symphony that is (consciously or unconsciously) declaring good news: The earth and everything in it is being restored, one step at a time, and that includes us as individuals. We are moving toward wholeness, and the fact that life evolves out of suffering and death means our pain is not wasted. In weakness offered humbly before God and man, we will be changed. Womb precedes birth, cross precedes resurrection, persecution precedes the spreading of the Church. Light emerges from the darkness.

Once we've begun to embrace our own weakness for the gift that it is, our entire worldview will be shaken up and rearranged — and only to our benefit. Where do we go now that everything is different? Where do we take this restless energy that beckons us into a renewed love affair with the world we live in? We've been changed, and we want to show it.

There's a famous line attributed to Saint Teresa of Calcutta, apparently spoken during her 1979 Nobel Peace Prize acceptance speech: "What can you do to promote world peace? Go home and love your family." I see this quote circulating around eight-by-ten-inch prints in Etsy shops and cross-stitched onto pillows. Its popular usage skyrockets among the young-mom demographic, no doubt because we desperately need encouragement that our unseen labor does in fact mean something for the greater good. But if you're at all familiar with the life and work of Mother Teresa — and most of us are — the pithy saying should feel a bit suspect.

And rightly so, because she never said it.

Mother Teresa's speech is recorded in the Nobel Prize archive, and what she actually said on the matter was this: "And so, my prayer for you is that truth will bring prayer in our homes, and from the foot of prayer will be that we believe that in the poor it is Christ. And we will really believe, we will begin to love. And we will love naturally, we will try to do something. *First in our own home, next door neighbor in the country we live, in the whole world.*"[17]

This humble saint never intended to advise us all to go home, love those who are our own, and call it a day: She said to start there, not to stop there. The distinction is critical.

But having said that, starting in your own home and with your own family is not only logical, it's necessary. We rightly sense the disorder present when hard inner work hasn't been done before we launch into external endeavors. Take, for example, a man with a reputation for good deeds and an impressive air of humanitarianism, but who with his wife is aloof and curt. Or a woman who works tirelessly for the welfare of children but refuses to forgive the offense of a family member. Or, ahem, an adoptive mom trying to heal early childhood trauma while coldly dismissing the expressed needs of her own husband. *Hypothetically.*

Unhealthy personal relationships do not necessarily detract from good things done, but the Lord desires our wholeness, not simply our works. When our closest relationships are lacking in love and virtue, they stand as glaring indicators that the gospel has not been allowed to have its perfect way in our hearts. After all, Jesus' life on earth points us not only to reconciliation with God but to reconciliation with our fellow man as well.

For this reason, we must look for transformation in our own homes and relationships before we can seek it in the world beyond our walls.

We cannot win the wrestling match to control those we love. We can try — God knows we do try; I have certainly tried my hardest — but the fight bears no fruit. Often, we assume the

---

17. Mother Teresa, transcript of Nobel Prize acceptance speech, December 10, 1979, https://www.nobelprize.org/nobel_prizes/peace/laureates/1979/teresa-acceptance_en.html, Italics added.

stance of a fighter without awareness of it. We crave control over our romantic partners, our children, our family of origin, our roommates; even the more naturally passive among us do it in our own unobtrusive way. Subconsciously (or sometimes, consciously) we believe that by retaining power we will protect ourselves from pain or discomfort, so we lace even our most intimate relationships with titanium. Just in case.

The gift that weakness offers is the invitation to strip it all off — the safety nets, the masks, the armor, the shields — and offer our true selves fully to another. When weakness paints us into a corner, we can choose authenticity. The exposure of our inner poverty invites us to shed the layer of protection we falsely assume serves us and to step into real freedom for perhaps the first time. This is the freedom to be fully known, as well as the freedom to feel compassion for those closest to us, those whose hurts so often rub raw our own.

To respond well to weakness, we must be willing to be vulnerable. This doesn't mean airing your dirty laundry on Facebook or to the stranger sitting next to you in church. Vulnerability requires a level of intimacy and trust that we cannot and will not share with all people. But those closest to us — family members, roommates, significant others, etc. — have likely already earned the right to be a confidant. We

> *Without putting ourselves at the mercy of another's compassion, we will never know what it is to be truly human.*

have the choice to let them in, which means expressing feelings that might embarrass us and fears that might debilitate us. There is always a chance of being misunderstood, which is part of what makes vulnerability feel like such a risk, but without putting ourselves at the mercy of another's compassion, we will never know what it is to be truly human.

Vulnerability comes more naturally to some than others, but it is required of all if we hope to nurture deep relationships with those around us. Powerful veneers might be impressive, but they are intrinsically separative too. You can never truly know someone with whom you don't feel equal, and you can never be truly known if you don't risk showing all your cards.

Can our own inner poverty be revealed and we respond poorly? Absolutely. It happens every day, and I'd wager most of our sins find their roots here. Responding in a healthy way to our weakness is always a choice, one that we are constantly making each day. There is no real "arrival" here, no threshold to cross after which you'll never fail to get it right. The exposure of our weakness is an invitation to committed transformation, to ongoing growth, not an instantaneous holiness infusion.

In her work in the field of shame and vulnerability, University of Houston research professor Dr. Brené Brown has found that meaningful human connection is our most primal need, and the fear of not having it is one of our most primitive motivators. In her book *Daring Greatly: How the Courage to Be Vulnerable Transforms the Way We Live, Love, Parent, and Lead*, Brown writes, "Connection, along with love and belonging (two expressions of connection), is why we are here, and it is what gives purpose and meaning to our lives." Speaking specifically of patterns that emerged from her research, she writes, "Shame is the fear of disconnection — it's the fear that something we've done or failed to do, an ideal that we've not lived up to, or a goal that we've not accomplished makes us unworthy of connection."[18] Shame, she says, motivates all of us; and the less we talk about it, the more control shame has.

This is not an easy conclusion to come to for many of us,

---

18. Brené Brown, *Daring Greatly: How the Courage to Be Vulnerable Transforms the Way We Live, Love, Parent, and Lead* (New York: Gotham Books, 2012), 68–69.

especially if we have not yet experienced a head-to-head collision with the reality of our weakness. Some of us may do a quick self-examination and conclude that, nope, we feel pretty darn lovable and worthy. *Our parents must have raised us right!*

But Brown's research shows that this shame is present even among those with elevated levels of confidence. We simply have different ways of coping with it, and some have learned to habitually repress fears of unworthiness, instead chasing down more pleasant or seemingly competent emotions. But this makes it clear: The fear of disconnection is a universal aspect of the human condition. We can grow in a positive way in how we respond to it, but no one is exempt.

When I examine the history of my own family life, I can see how this longing for connection — and anxiety of not receiving it — has played a big role. In the most challenging years of new parenthood, I feared I was doomed to a future of disconnection from both my husband and my son, and many days I responded to that fear by desperately grasping for control. Whether taking it upon myself to relieve Eric's anxiety or demanding our son comply with my rigid expectations, I was

If we hope to live out the affirmation of human dignity in the world, we must start with those closest to us.

constantly exhausting myself with a burden of control that was never mine to carry. As the years go by, I am slowly learning to "let go and let God," as they say, but it is a work in progress as I continually practice remembering that the only one I can control is myself.

Catholic teaching is consistent in its adherence to the dignity of the human person. From the Bible to the *Catechism of the Catholic Church*, this belief permeates and shapes both our theology and our corporate response to it. In the introduction to his encyclical *Evangelium Vitae* ("The Gospel of Life"), Pope Saint John Paul II wrote of "the wonderful truth recalled by the Second Vatican Council: 'By his incarnation the Son of God has united himself in some fashion with every human being.' This saving event reveals to humanity not only the boundless love of God who 'so loved the world that he gave his only Son' (Jn 3:16), but also the incomparable value of every human person. ... The Gospel of God's love for man, the Gospel of the dignity of the person and the Gospel of life are a single and indivisible Gospel."[19]

Everything a baptized person does on any given day should uphold the recognition that the body, soul, and spirit of each person is sacred precisely because that person has been made in the image of God and shares in the humanity he took on in the Incarnation. This belief should inform our politics, our worldviews, and our moral codes. But perhaps it is never so challenging to live out as in the day-to-day of our mundane family interactions. The more distanced a person is from ourselves, the less messy our engagement with them will probably be, while our most complicated relationships are often with those under our own roof. But if we hope to live out the affirmation of human dignity in the world, we must start with those closest to us.

Personally, I have a harder time accepting this dignity in children than in adults, and I don't think I'm alone in this. Perhaps it's because a mature person's relationship to a child — particularly our own — necessarily involves a fair amount of guiding and teaching and putting up with some general nonsense. (As a friend once joked to me, "If any other roommate threw a tantrum over putting on his shoes, he would be the biggest jerk in the world.") But perhaps it's because the human heart craves power, and children are vulnerable targets. You can get away with a lot of bossing

19. Pope Saint John Paul II, *Evangelium Vitae*, March 25, 1995, http://w2.vatican.va/content/john-paul-ii/en/encyclicals/documents/hf_jp-ii_enc_25031995_evangelium-vitae.html, 2.

a child around that you wouldn't dare try with anyone else. We somehow feel we are entitled to control children.

For this reason, I am impressed by those adults who practice honoring the dignity of children. Recently at a baptism in my parish, a big brother in attendance was just a little too excited about his sister's sacrament, bouncing around as children are wont to do and creating a minor distraction. The wise priest wordlessly and gently gave the boy the important task of holding the Sacramentary while the priest read from it. The boy did a great job, distractions ceased, and all of us watching were reminded that the child was a fellow human being, not an animal to be subdued and controlled.

The godmother of one of my sons is very intentional about referring to the children in her life as her "friends," and not in a wink-wink kind of way. "My friend Candace, who is ten, loves horses," she'll say seriously. It's awkward sometimes, as though there's a peanut-chomping elephant in the room, but it points me to the dignity of children every single time. I am challenged and grateful.

But you may have noticed that both of those examples, the two that immediately came to mind for me, are of people who do not actually have children themselves. It is laudable but not exceedingly difficult to honor the dignity of a child when you get to go home later and read a book or eat a full meal uninterrupted. Parenting is an intense road to sanctification, and the ride is a bumpy one.

People are not ours to control, and our own children should not be an exception. Parents have the obligation to keep their children (and others, through their actions) safe and guide them in wise decision-making; but at the end of the day we cannot control them. And sometimes it seems the harder a parent tries, the worse things get. It serves us well to keep at the forefront of our minds that our children ultimately belong to the Lord and are not little automatons built to feed our egos.

In his kindness, God gives us this baptism-by-fire right out of the gate. Anyone who has had a newborn has wrestled mightily with the desire to control versus the inability to do so. How we respond to this predicament matters greatly: It can potentially set the stage for how the next few (or twenty) years will go. If we clench our fists stubbornly and refuse to compromise or give an inch, we are likely to remain in this fight-or-flight posture until our child's prefrontal cortex has finished developing. *Warning: This is a long time.*

Parenting is a spiritual practice in more ways than one, and developing the habit of non-attachment to our goals and expectations — not to our child, to whom I hope we are extremely attached — is one of its greatest gifts. If we unclench our proverbial fists and manage to open up our palms, we have access to greater peace and can work creatively on solutions that respect the personhood of both parent and child.

But the principle of relinquishing the desire for control is not relegated to children. On the contrary, it's just as applicable to every relationship we have. If you don't believe me, take an honest assessment of the state of your insides at the next family gathering and tell me you don't find yourself wanting the adults in your life to conform to your own ways of being. Stick around long enough after the plates are cleared and you won't be able to not notice it.

Personally, I have observed that my heart rate quickens when my parents make choices I wouldn't have, or my adult siblings express opinions that differ from mine. My body tenses when Eric's autonomy tweaks the strings of my inner peace yet again. But in these moments, I have choices of my own: I can choose to remember the boundaries of my own personhood and, equally as important, choose to respect theirs as well. We are different people, and we have to learn to honor differences rather than feel threatened by them.

You are not in control. Isn't that one of the most difficult but potentially freeing truths of our lives? There are very few things we can legitimately control, and, frankly, most have to do with how we respond to the things we can't. People are not ours to control. Part of the inherent dignity of the human person is that we are each unique, and as such each of us has the right to our own thoughts, beliefs, methodology, and opinions.

Psychologist Carl Jung coined the term "individuation" to describe the life process of differentiating between the personal and collective unconscious to find who we are as an individual rather than who we are as part of a crowd. While at times it feels like it would be easier if everyone in our inner circle could just engage in some robotic group think, the reality would be horrifying. I must do my own hard inner work of making peace with the uniqueness of myself, and I must allow you to do the same. It is only then that we can live healthily together. But this is not my instinct My instinct is to make you *me*. I must learn to unclench my fists.

The counselor held my gaze longer than I wished she would. What did I want? I wanted optimism back. I wanted the naïveté of assuming we would live happily ever after with a mostly satisfying family life full of impish kids who committed the occasional "aw, shucks" offense. I wanted back the days when coming home felt like reprieve and not strain. I wanted things to have turned out the way I thought they would. I wanted my husband to be exactly who I thought he was when we married, and I wanted to be that for him.

I wanted it all to be easier.

"Does it really matter what I want?" I snapped. "This is what we have."

Eric shifted in his seat beside mine, and I thought I sensed his disapproval at my tone, but when I looked up, his expression matched my own. For all the struggle of the past few years, we still understood one another better than anyone. Against all odds, we were still best friends. That counted for something.

I sighed, "I want to know that God is in this."

"Do you doubt it?" the counselor asked.

I wanted to smack her sweet, pink, newly engaged cheeks. What did she know of hardship? I swallowed the lump in my throat and nodded instead. Instantly, I knew I was lying. Luke 6:43–44 swam through my head: "No good tree bears bad fruit, nor again does a bad tree bear good fruit; for each tree is known by its own fruit." What was the fruit of this?

My husband was still here. Our vows had been upheld through hell and high water.

Though motherhood felt like a drowning, my love for my sons never left.

Each time sorrow lasted for a night, joy came in the morning. Sometimes even laughter. (If you're looking for God, I've heard, you need to listen for laughter.)

I had stopped judging people almost entirely; mercy had finally triumphed over judgment.

I felt my need for God more than ever before, even as I wondered where he was.

Our brokenness had allowed us to receive the comfort of a homeless community.

Being needy for others had snuffed out my pride.

I had met Jesus in the weakness of his Incarnation, and I called him brother.

I had met Jesus in the suffering of his Passion, and I called him friend.

Life was hard, yes, but it was good and true and beautiful as well. The valleys were dark and dreadful things, but, if I had eyes to see it, the mountains were nearer to heaven than I could have once imagined. I was learning to release control, to admit that perhaps I could hold the tension between everything I had expected and everything I had gotten, and be grateful for it all.

"No," I choked out a whisper. "No, I don't doubt this is God at all."

Chapter Seven

TRANSFORMATION
IN THE WORLD

We stepped out the doors of the church, the smell of incense still in our nostrils, the strength of the aroma a particular favorite of our sensory-seeking preschooler. Never had I enjoyed attending church more than I did lately, bookending a pew full of the quirkiest cast of characters this parish had ever seen. People may think devout Catholics all look and act a certain way, but stretched out across the wooden seats next to us were those in dingy clothes, cheap tattoos, unwashed hair, and enormous grins. Maybe some did fall asleep every week, but regardless, every week we were there — a part of the faithful. I hadn't even tried to hide a wry smile that morning when bodies swayed overenthusiastically as the closing hymn jogged along at a peppy pace. Mass with this crew was a joy.

It was a rare Sunday that found both my husband and me able to sit all the way through the liturgy with our two wiggly boys, even with a dozen willing hands to help on all sides. But, somehow, we had successfully made it through the entirety of this Mass and there was an extra skip in my step as we left the narthex.

Our group had just begun dividing ourselves up into vans when we were approached on the sidewalk. Dressed in well-starched slacks, coordinating heels, and a silk blouse, a woman flashed an eager smile that betrayed the novelty she found in her present company. None of us knew her, but we gamely maintained a pleasant conversation about the weather and the day's homily, trying to give her time to say what was on her mind.

Finally, she turned to Tina and extended a good-natured pat to one exposed, weathered shoulder. "We're glad you're here!" she announced to my clearly impoverished friend. "You are welcome in church anytime!"

Tina's eyes lit up. "Well thank you," she cackled wildly. "So are you!"

The God of my childhood imagination was a strong, old, white man; something of a cross between Zeus and King Triton from Disney's *The Little Mermaid*. He sat on a throne and oozed power. I knew he was loving, but equally that he was not to be trifled with. I attended enough Sunday morning services to learn the word "smote."

It's okay to see God this way for a while — appropriate, even, for a certain life stage. But as our minds and spirits evolve, our understanding of the Trinity should, too. For one thing, "father" can mean many things to us, depending on our respective life experiences and the culture in which we were raised. When I lived in Indonesia, it was common to see men peacefully pacing up and down our alley wearing *sarongs* around their waists and babies in *selendangs* tied over their shoulders. This is one of my favorite images of fatherhood; I can still see their smiles of gentle pride and affection in my mind's eye.

But instead of drawing from the tenderness of the archetypal father, cultural Christianity has long emphasized the power of a father. Instead of calling attention to the inclusivity and security that a daddy provides his children, our version of God the Father is drenched in exclusivity and conditional love. You might argue that this hasn't been your personal experience with Christianity — and I hope it hasn't — but an honest look at our history and overarching culture sadly upholds this. It is subtler than we think.

> *Once we have allowed our weakness to transform our own hearts and relationships, the implications will inevitably extend to the outside world.*

Why does this discrepancy exist? Why, when there are so many nurturing qualities of fatherhood to draw from, have we collectively over-fixated on God's authority and might? The gospel makes it clear that God is more concerned with the world knowing his love than his ability to send them to hell. Why can't we seem to feel the same? A strong argument can be made that Emperor Constantine is to blame, since his rule was the first to mix the gospel with political power. But that would let the rest of us off the hook, I'm afraid, and the truth is more personal than that.

We elevate the characteristics of God that are mighty and impressive because it makes us feel safe; and not only safe, but powerful, because the idea of walking through life vulnerable to forces outside our control is a terrifying one. How much more comforting it is to assure ourselves that we are on the winning team — undeniably more comfortable than the possibility that there are no teams after all. But Jesus' Incarnation and Passion stubbornly refuse to let us stay there. It's inconvenient, really, how his example points us back to the value of our frailty and sufferings. His humanity pulls us out of our own self-importance to reintroduce us to the world he gave up everything to be united to.

Once we have allowed our weakness to transform our own hearts and relationships, the implications will inevitably extend to the outside world. It can't *not* do so, because now more than ever we understand that we are connected to all things, and all things to us, and have learned that having compassion on ourselves pours out to others. We then have a decision to make about the narrative we choose to join: Will we continue on with a paradigm of a Christian calling to correct, judge, and hold the world around us at a distance? Or will we see others as sisters and brothers, agreeing with Jesus that it is good and true to share a humanity with broken people?

The American church, Protestant and Catholic alike, has become defensive. (I am a citizen of the United States, so this is the specific Christian culture I can speak to, but perhaps those in other nations are falling prey to the same end.) We are afraid of religious freedom being taken from us, but we are unwilling to consider how we've done the same to others. We are angry that our society is shifting to post-Christianity, but we ignore how bad "the good old days" were for so many. We claim to be maligned and persecuted, but we might just be lying in a bed of our own making.

Gregory Boyle, a Jesuit priest and founder of Homeboy Industries, a mission which helps rehabilitate former gang members in Los Angeles, says it best in his book *Barking to the Choir: The Power of Radical Kinship*:

> In a recent *New Yorker* profile of American Baptists, the congregation's leadership resigned itself to the fact that "secular culture" would always be "hostile" to Christianity. I don't believe this is true. Our culture is hostile only to the inauthentic living of the gospel. It sniffs out hypocrisy everywhere and knows when Christians aren't taking seriously what Jesus took seriously. It is, by and large, hostile to the right things. It actually longs to embrace the gospel of inclusion and nonviolence, of compassionate love and acceptance. Even atheists cherish such a prospect.[20]

We are at a pivotal point in history. It's time to rethink the Church's relationship to the world and the message we are sending. Do we really want it to be one of antagonism, in which we are suspicious and fearful of anyone who isn't exactly like us? Or are we ready to dare to live incarnationally, modeling our lives more after the tender, historical Jesus and less after a colonial ideal of a power-infused god of victory?

Letting our weakness transform us will always result in a theology of reciprocity. By that I mean an understanding of God and the

---

20. Gregory Boyle, SJ, *Barking to the Choir: The Power of Radical Kinship* (New York: Simon & Schuster, 2017), 2.

universe that acknowledges a constant flow between the positions we allow one another to take: wounded and healer, teacher and learner, expert and novice, needy and giver. Our place in the world is ever-changing and nuanced, and the dignity of mankind is that we are all capable of playing every part. This necessarily changes the way we interact with others and the way we do ministry and missions. If we encounter our own weakness in the light of the Holy Spirit, the layers of self-preservation will gradually be broken down until, truly, all is grace. Recognizing the poverty within ourselves means we are better receptacles of the riches of others.

This is not to say that the revelation of our shared weakness does away with socioeconomic realities. Admitting that I have a deep internal poverty does not negate the fact that others are living in physical poverty, and that this is a cross I do not carry. In middle- to upper-class Christian circles, you are likely to hear sentiments like, "There are a lot of ways to be poor." What is meant by this, of course, is that physical poverty is not the only way a person can ache, and some of the richest individuals in the world are also the most emotionally and relationally bankrupt. What is meant is that everyone has endured some degree of suffering, and many well-to-do people are carrying deep wounds that we as Christians are called to have compassion on and to reach out to. This is all absolutely true, and I don't argue against it.

But behind the words that are said is often a spirit of wrongly equalizing all kinds of poverty, as though justice for those who literally have less is not particularly important, and the fact that life is easy for no one makes obsolete the fact that it is still easier for some than others. The gospel of Jesus Christ obliterates the invisible divide between us, yes, but it also calls us forth to be obliterators of the visible divides as well — and we can't do that while denying those divides exist.

The Catholic Church teaches a "preferential option for the poor," which Pope Saint Paul VI described this way in one of his apostolic letters: "The Gospel instructs us in the preferential respect due to the poor and the special situation they have in society: the more fortunate should renounce some of their rights so as to place their goods more generously at the service of others."[21]

As difficult as that may be to swallow, the implications are clear: Christians have a responsibility to live our lives in service of the physically poor. While not denying or belittling other real types of needs, Christians are specifically called to seek justice for those who have been positioned by circumstance and society to have less and struggle more.

A popular argument against this theology is that "coddling" the marginalized only keeps them reliant upon handouts, and therefore only results in an undermining of their dignity. While this can be true at times, it is no excuse to throw the baby out with the bathwater. On the contrary, we have all the more responsibility to work toward solutions that affirm the dignity of the poor even as we go out of our way to come alongside them.

If this sounds counterproductive — if extending particular concern for the poor seems only to solidify our differences rather than bring unity between us all — consider the conclusion drawn by the United States Conference of Catholic Bishops. In a 1986 pastoral letter entitled "Economic Justice for All," the bishops said that the purpose of a preferential option for the poor is "to enable all persons to share in and contribute to the common good … not an adversarial slogan that pits one group or class against another. Rather it states that the deprivation and powerlessness of the poor wounds the whole community. The extent of their suffering is a measure of how far we are from being a true community of persons. These wounds will be healed only by greater solidarity with the poor and among the poor themselves."[22]

---

21. Pope Paul VI, *Octogesima Adveniens*, May 14, 1971, http://w2.vatican.va/content/paul-vi/en/apost_letters/documents/hf_p-vi_apl_19710514_octogesima-adveniens.html, 23.

22. United States Conference of Catholic Bishops, *Economic Justice for All*, November, 1986, http://www.usccb.org/upload/economic_justice_for_all.pdf, 88.

"The deprivation ... of the poor wounds the whole community." This is another way of saying we are all connected; we belong to one another, and the ordering of our lives around the plight of the poor is central to our Christian faith.

I have found that many Christians avoid real, hands-on interaction with those who battle poverty by claiming that it isn't safe, or that they are afraid of what their children might be exposed to. There is a fear threshold that must be crossed here, and there's simply no way to do it other than running in headfirst. In my own experience, and in listening to the experience of many others, our worst fears are very rarely founded. So much of it is simply a fear of the unknown. Sure, things are messy, but with wisdom and discernment, it is perfectly possible to engage marginalized communities or persons without significantly compromising the health and safety of yourself or your loved ones. Will you be uncomfortable? It's quite likely. But comfort and safety are two very different things, and there are plenty of ways to challenge the former without endangering the latter. At the same time, we acknowledge that following Jesus does necessitate a certain amount of risk. That's why it's called faith.

If we let it, our weakness can deliver us from judgment and replace it with awe.

If we have the courage to examine our fears honestly, we are likely to find that they are rooted in judgments we have against those of a lower socioeconomic class. No one likes to admit to making such judgments, but it's important to be truthful with ourselves. While some stereotypes may prove accurate, Jesus calls us to see past outward behaviors and look at the heart. The problem is that we can't look at someone's heart unless we're close enough to them to take a peek.

Only once we've identified our unfair judgments can we move

past our fears, but if we don't have the courage to admit the truth, we're stuck. Father Boyle, whom I quoted earlier, casts the vision best in his best-selling book, *Tattoos on the Heart*: "Here is what we seek: a compassion that can stand in awe of what the poor have to carry rather than stand in judgment at how they carry it."[23]

If we let it, our weakness can deliver us from judgment and replace it with awe.

When we consider how making peace with our personal weakness could ever impact the world, it may feel ludicrous to believe it matters. We are small drops in the bucket, yes, but physics teaches us that every bucket has a point of overflow. We must overcome the temptation to despair. If we are going to see God's kingdom come on earth as it is in heaven, we must be willing to build it, brick by brick.

Embracing our weakness necessarily shifts our posture in the world. Rather than believing we have the solution to the problem, we now understand that we are part of the problem itself. This may sound hopeless, but if you have been changed by embracing your poverty, the odds are you've never felt more hopeful. Before, we may have said our hope was in Christ alone, but our hearts and actions testified otherwise. In truth, our hope was primarily in being right and convincing others of the fact. Now, when we say our hope is in Christ alone, we are confessing our insufficiencies and lack of answers. We are free.

This freedom causes us to fall in love with the world around us. When we no longer feel bound to see the world as us and them, we begin to notice divine love showing up everywhere. How impertinent of God, acting in and through people and places we always thought we needed to bring to him. Who knew that he had been there all along, just waiting for us to join in the fun?

There is no place on earth where God is absent. As my four-

---

23. Gregory Boyle, *Tattoos on the Heart: The Power of Boundless Compassion* (New York: Free Press, 2010), 67.

year-old observed this past Easter, "The only place that God is not is in the tomb!" But this doesn't negate the fact that our work and partnership are still needed; on the contrary, the ones who can honor the image of God in their fellow humans are the ones needed most. We still have a call to live out the works of mercy and share the love of Christ. The difference is that now we do it as equals, as comrades, as fellow sojourners, rather than as superiors and — let's be honest — know-it-alls.

We are charged with finding creative solutions for the needs of marginalized communities that are in keeping with their human dignity, rather than rushing to solve problems in ways that seem fast and effective from our ignorant perspective. This necessitates giving extensively of our time and attention to learn about the needs of a community and how to equip the community members to meet those needs themselves:

> Since there are so many people prostrate with hunger in the world, this sacred council urges all, both individuals and governments, to remember the aphorism of the Fathers, "Feed the man dying of hunger, because if you have not fed him, you have killed him," and really to share and employ their earthly goods, according to the ability of each, *especially by supporting individuals or peoples with the aid by which they may be able to help and develop themselves.*[24]

A friend of mine who spent years working in Haiti told me that after the catastrophic earthquake struck in 2010, peanut butter was one of the top products donated by the United States. While

---

24. Second Vatican Council, *Gaudium et Spes* (*Pastoral Constitution on the Church in the Modern World*), December 7, 1965, http://www.vatican.va/archive/hist_councils/ii_vatican_council/documents/vat-ii_const_19651207_gaudium-et-spes_en.html, 69, Italics added.

we assumed the protein-packed food was saving lives, we were oblivious to the fact that half a million Haitians earn their livelihood from peanut production. Our efforts to help alleviate hunger actually put indigenous people out of work, simply because we didn't take the time to assess what the needs were or how we could utilize the local economy to meet them. The book *When Helping Hurts: How to Alleviate Poverty without Hurting the Poor ... And Yourself* does an excellent job of unpacking this topic.

But it isn't just large international operations that demand these conversations. The same thoughtful analysis is necessary in our local endeavors as well. We can't help people if we don't know what they need, and we can't know what they need without knowing the people. We must listen closely and elevate the voices of the marginalized. We must ask not only, "What do you need?" but also, "How can I serve you as you pursue a solution?" It is time we restructured our approach from the ground up.

Many of us feel unsure of how to go about restructuring our personal lives to reflect a value of solidarity. Even if we have let our weakness begin to transform us, many of us are still living just like we did in the past. Should we sell all our belongings and travel the globe as missionaries? Should we join a religious order or take a vow of poverty? Some of us will be called to those things, but most won't. For most, living out an incarnational faith will not mean making one huge decision that will change lives overnight; rather, it means making dozens of little decisions every day that change us — and our world — over the long haul.

If you don't know where to start, I suggest evaluating where you spend most of your time. It may even help to get out a pen and start writing. Depending on your lifestyle, vocation, and season of life, this short list may look different from one person to the next, but here are some examples to get your wheels turning:

- Home
- Work
- School
- Dorm
- Church
- Volunteer commitments
- Small group/Bible study
- Book club
- Child's school or extracurriculars
- Favorite restaurants or coffee shops

Next, think about the people you spend the most time with in these places. Consider whether you are invested in those relationships in a give-and-take capacity. Could you change your approach in a way that might better honor the other's dignity? Notice what kinds of people you spend the most time with. Are they more or less just like you? Have you tried to invite outsiders into these familiar places? (Most of us could do a better job of surrounding ourselves with diversity. If an honest assessment of these questions feels embarrassing or convicting, resist the urge to shrink back in discouragement and instead simply determine to be more intentional from here on out.)

Now that you've identified where and with whom you spend most of your time, take a good look at what you've written down. More than likely, a vast majority of your chance to live out the gospel will be found in these places, not in a fantasy life you dream of in which you have more hours in the day and different life circumstances to make it easier, or in some distant reality when you finally commit to all of those outreach opportunities you've been meaning to take on. This, right here, is your life: This is what you have to work with today. Don't waste time waiting for tomorrow.

With this in mind, brainstorm a list of changes you could make to better live out the principles of solidarity and a preferential option for the poor. How could you incorporate the works of mercy into your life in a natural and dignity-affirming way? This list might look something like this:

- Taking your children to a park in a low-income part of town and getting to know families whose experience differs from yours
- Choosing to patron restaurants owned by immigrants rather than your favorite chain, and perhaps building relationships with the owners while giving them your support
- Using public transportation to literally rub shoulders with people you normally wouldn't and get some valuable perspective on their realities
- Considering how to deepen the relationships already in your life that you could invest in — a lonely person at work, an international student in your class, a neighbor who doesn't quite fit in, etc.
- Being open to changing jobs (or, if you're a student, mindfully choosing a major or job) if the calling arises
- Intentionally inviting others with whom you wouldn't normally spend time with to your home for dinner. You don't have to know them well to extend the invitation — that's the point of the meal! Remember, eating together is a great equalizer.

This is just the tip of the iceberg, but hopefully it gets you started. Remember, all any of us has is our little corner of the world, and in that corner nothing is too small to matter.

———————

It had been a hard day. We still had them sometimes — the bad ones — though with so much support they were becoming fewer and farther between. I stumbled wearily out to the living room after putting both boys to bed and smiled halfheartedly at Cathy, who was sitting on the couch. *She needs you,* I thought to myself, *you've got to get it together for her.* Swallowing the lump in my throat, I sank into the faded red cushions beside her.

"How are you?" I asked, sincerely wanting to know. Cathy's mental health was often fragile; she was an incredible woman of resourcefulness and compassion, but one who battled the residual effects of a traumatic childhood. If anyone knew a thing or two about a bad day, it was Cathy. I could vent about my own later to my husband, his tender arms around me in our soft, warm bed. Cathy would be sleeping alone in her Buick tonight. She deserved a listening ear.

"Oh me? I'm fine." She said it with the breezy air of a woman who's never had a care in the world, before letting her eyes settle in on me. "I'm worried about you."

I started to deflect the statement with a wave of my hand, then stopped. I remembered a few weeks before when we had sat in the backyard and watched the kids play, remembered the strange, sweet words Cathy had said. "Thank you for sharing your family with me," she said with a smile. Nothing in particular had happened, we had just been there, sitting in chairs. Sitting like a regular old day.

I knew I had a decision to make. I could give Cathy the nice, shiny version of myself, assuring her that all was fine and piously recounting my blessings. I could save the vulnerability for those "like me" later on — in the dark with my husband, on the phone with a college friend. Or I could give Cathy what she deserved: the truth. I could give her the dignity of being an emotional refuge for me. I could wage war against the idea that she was unworthy to be my confidant.

Drawing in my breath, I confessed my failures and my fears, my inadequacies and my despair. "I will never be mother enough for this," I whimpered to her. "I feel trapped, scared. I don't know how to do this right, and I'm afraid of failing for the rest of my life." I wiped my wet cheeks as the words spilled out.

Cathy had a habit of putting a throw pillow on her lap when she sat. She drew the nearest one in now, hands and elbows working to mold it into her stomach as she thought about what I had said. "Listen," she urged, "you are a great mom. This is really hard — your circumstances are hard — but you love those boys so much. It will get easier. You're really doing a great job."

Her feedback was simple — so simple, in fact, I likely would've snubbed it coming from someone else. But from Cathy, it meant something. She had suffered. She had known hardship. If Cathy, who had survived an abusive childhood, single parenting, homelessness, and physical disability, said my circumstances were hard, then hell, I believed her. She gave a validation birthed from experience that no one else in my life was positioned to offer. She gave me what no one else could.

Cathy launched into stories about raising her own son, affection and heartache dripping from her tongue. Sitting there beside her, listening to yarns spun, my mind's eye zoomed out like a wide lens and I saw the last decade of my life and the unlikely trajectory it had taken.

That girl who went to Indonesia to save the world had crashed and burned. Thank God for it — for lighting the whole thing on fire and standing with me in silence as the flames licked my heels. I had loved others, but had never bled with them; I had believed they belonged to me, but could never understand how I belonged to them. It was all dust now. I stood over the ashes of my old self, knowing I'd been changed, lingering in the soot and the smoke, letting my wounds show, letting my humanity bind me, letting the ones people called "lost" hold me tight. Realizing I had been found.

EPILOGUE

We were gathered outside on a late spring night, warm with the lingering presence of the Texas sun, bellies full of Indian curry and crusty homemade bread. We sat on hay bales, we sat on hastily hammered-together benches, we paced around the patchy grass, some of us needing a smoke but finding none. We sat beside who we were *with*, and someone handed him a guitar.

His brown fingers plucked the strings and the fragrant Latino music curled to the sky like incense. The song had no words, but the night couldn't possibly have contained any. We held our breath because something was happening, we knew not what. Tina's grandmothered hips began to sway. Faces cracked smiles because they loved Tina. Faces rolled eyes because they hated Tina. One hand found the other and she raised them above her head.

Clap-clap. Clap-clap.

Red tank top and too-short shorts began spinning, the long, wrinkled legs twirling underneath. Who knew if she'd been drinking? She was beautiful.

The air began to change and we looked around at one another's faces, wondering if the others felt it too. What choice do you have in the second that hinges the temporal with the eternal? Only a fool would retreat. We took a breath.

There is only so much beauty a moment can contain, and when it reaches its fullness, it will pop like a balloon. Often the pieces float up into thin air, leaving you grasping at wind, desperately crying out for beauty's return. But once in a while the substance falls around you rather than rising above, and beauty multiplies rather than escapes. We don't get to choose when the popping will occur, and the unpredictability is part of the miracle. Rarely will it happen at a candlelit dinner on Valentine's Day, but don't be surprised if you feel the pieces linger on your palms when you find your children's limbs curled around each other at 11:36 p.m. on an unsuspecting Thursday night.

Shards of this beauty landed on us all like an alcoholic fairy's dust. We were intoxicated.

Clap-clap. Clap-clap.

Heaven itself had come down to keep the rhythm with her.

The invitation had been extended. I swayed, the baby tucked in snug against my breasts in an olive-green sling. And one by one we gave in to the evening; one by one we all started to dance.

When you dance face to face with other human beings, there are things that fall away: college diplomas, prison records, reputations, social statuses, trauma histories, biggest failures, greatest successes — that is, all the imaginary lines that we draw between *you* and *me*. The walls disappear when you clap your hands together to the rhythm of a Spanish guitar. Then it's up to you to choose whether they are allowed to return when the last note rises into the night.

Timidly, body gently swaying in time, Rachel asked to hold the baby. She had told me over dinner that he reminded her of her grandson, whom she rarely got to see. Rachel was twenty-six years old.

Tenderly, I unwrapped my floppy infant and placed him in my friend's freckled hands. She lifted him up, soft head against her soft shoulder, and murmured something in his ear as her knees kept the beat.

Some of us are broken by our children and some of us are healed by them, and I can make nothing of it except to pass my baby around and let other women smell his hair. There is something in the fragrance of lavender shampoo and spit up that keeps us from giving up hope.

I lifted the empty sling over my head and was met with the awkward freedom that mothers of nurslings experience when another cradles our child. My eyes scanned the circle in search of my oldest son, and I chuckled with delight to watch his flailing arms going one way, legs another. Contrary to the laws of genetics, the child seemed to have inherited my own sense of rhythm. Moving toward him, I stretched out my arms to my son. His chocolate fingers wrapped around my vanilla ones and he jumped up and down, nearly pulling my arms out of their sockets, always his "dance" of preference. We lurched around to the music and laughed together at the ridiculous results. Occasionally I would look up to see my friends' smiles, to see them clapping despite themselves or cheering us on. They were living lives largely devoid of the presence of children, and our bizarre dance was a good gift.

It occurred to me that my son and I might be thinking the very same thing: *Finally, here, I belong.* And it occurred to me that maybe all of us there could be thinking the very same thing. Jewish philosopher Martin Buber said the "I" finds its fullness in the "thou."[25] I read that over a decade ago, but have only just begun to see that it's the only way I ever want to live.

The strings crooned, the notes rose, and the night should

25. Martin Buber, *I and Thou* (Martino Publishing, 2010; originally published in 1923; first English translation published in 1937).

have never ended, but time doesn't heed our "shoulds." We drove home, and I lay beside my son in his bed, the way I did every night, his forty pounds nestled tight under the blanket with the pastel foxes playing in the river.

I and thou, kid, I thought to myself as I stroked his forehead under the icon of the Mother of God of Tenderness. His daddy had chosen it for his room because of the rich skin of Mary and the Christ Child, little brown fingers tenderly draped around the neck of the Mother of God incarnate. They walked such earth. Did they dance such dances? That fragile child grew to dwell among the poor and the needy, to find his home with them. He, lonely and despised, knew what it was to share their groan.

I watched as dark eyes grew heavy, felt the breathing of tiny lungs grow steady, and I whispered a choked thanksgiving for the mercy it took to let me hear that music play.

And he is still plucking the strings, inviting us to hold tight to one another and dance reckless in cigarette-speckled grass. He plays on, dizzying us with notes that demand a spinning, that demand a breaking, that demand a love that will expand when it thinks it can no longer. He plays on, bidding us not to take our eyes off one another, not to stop the dance.

And there is ever more room in the circle.

DISCUSSION
QUESTIONS

1. Where do you recognize the desire for power or competency in your own life? Do you feel pressured not to let weakness show (professionally, socially, spiritually, as a parent, etc.)?

2. What are the "numbing agents" that you find yourself reaching for to self-medicate the loneliness, disappointments, or sufferings in your life? What would it require for you to give those up? With what could you replace them?

3. Shannon writes of her past view of God as being one of strict power and authority, and how it shifted to one of solidarity and compassion when she encountered Jesus in his Incarnation during her time of need. How would you describe your own view of God, both now and in the past? How have your life experiences impacted your relationship with God?

4. In times of your own suffering, have you found refuge in Jesus' passion? If not, what messages from our culture might have kept you from meeting Jesus there?

5. Look back on your experiences of ministry, volunteer work, acts of service, etc. Do you think the structures in place, no matter how well-intentioned, created a power dynamic that made an "us" and "them" out of those serving and those being served? What would it look like to engage in this work in

a way that better affirms the dignity of all parties?

6. Think of a time when someone opened up vulnerably to you about a trial in their life that you personally had never experienced. Did hearing their story spark an empathetic response in you? Going forward, did it change the way you perceived other people facing that trial? How does this apply to the importance of embracing your own places of weakness?

7. Our weakness is on display in our homes perhaps more than anywhere, and often our response is to seek to control our family members, roommates, and significant others. How does the instinct to control show up in your life? What would happen in these relationships if you began to unclench your fists?

8. In the last chapter, Shannon guided you through making a list of ideas for how to practice solidarity and belonging within the natural rhythms of your own life. Did you have any ideas that sparked hope within you? How could you live out the inclusivity of Jesus in the everyday life you already lead?

Acknowledgments

Neither this book nor the transformation of my heart would exist without the quiet life's work of Jean Vanier and his commitment to the gospel of weakness. To him I offer humble gratitude and the feeble hope that I might be a worthy mouthpiece to carry on his message. Likewise, this work would not exist without the rigorous research, practical application, and gentle delivery of the late Dr. Karyn Purvis and her team at Texas Christian University. Mine is not the first nor the last adoptive family she has saved, and I eagerly join in the chorus of voices grateful for her dedication to healing trauma. Likewise, I am grateful to the Empowered to Connect ministry of Irving Bible Church in Irving, Texas, for formatting Dr. Purvis' material in an accessible and explicitly Christian way for struggling parents.

My story would not be what it is without those whose paths have intersected with my own. I am grateful for my teammates in Indonesia — the Perrys, the Hetlands, the Buckners, the O'Quins, and the Gibsons — and the generous way they accompanied my husband and me on our journeys; for our family, the O'Brien and the Evans sides, and the unending source of love and support they have provided over the years; and perhaps especially for my father, who bears the guilt of my genetic insatiability for written words.

I am grateful for our friends at the Denton Catholic Worker, both those who remain and those who have, like us, moved on. You gave me some of the happiest times of my life and showed me a glimpse of what this world could be. I love you all.

Our friends and parish community at St. Thomas Aquinas have not only loved our family well but have cheered me on personally as a writer, too. A special thank you to Father Jon Seda, who was the first to thrust me alone before a crowd to talk about suffering because he believed my voice mattered before I did.

If this manuscript is at all above sub-par, it is because of the sharp eye and generous spirit of my editor, Mary Beth Baker, to whom I am indebted.

I don't enjoy thinking about the person I would be had I not married Eric Evans. This book is for him, because he keeps wonder and mystery ever before me. He is the love of my life.

And, finally, of course, our children. Only two are in this book, but each is represented here. They have broken me, healed me, and have saved my humanity. It is for their sakes (and the sakes of all our children) that I want to see the world changed.

About the Author

Shannon K. Evans has always found God by putting words on paper. Her writing has been featured in *America*, *St. Anthony Messenger*, and *Tapestry* magazines as well as numerous places online, including *Huffington Post*, RelevantMagazine.com, *Sick Pilgrim*, and *Verily*. She has authored *Bearing Light*, an Advent devotional for Blessed Is She, and has contributed to the books *When We Were Eve: Uncovering the Woman God Created You to Be* (Franciscan Media, 2017) and *Rally: Litanies for the Lovers of God and Neighbor* (Upper Room Books, 2019). Shannon, her husband, and their five children enjoy slow living in small-town Iowa. To follow her writing or book a speaking engagement, visit her website at www.shannonkevans.com.